I0824578

SMOKE AND SEASONED BREAD

HASAN SEMAY

SMOKE AND SEASONED BREAD

RECIPES FROM TÜRKIYE

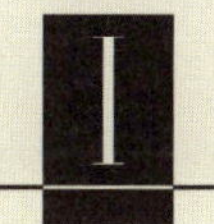

Interlink Books
An imprint of Interlink Publishing Group, Inc.

DEPARTURE 6

THE BASICS 14
BEYOGLU 16

MEZE 30
ISTANBUL 32

FISH 72
KUMKAPI 74

VEG 102
TRABZON 104

BREAD 134
DIYARBAKIR 136

MEAT 156
URFA 158

DESSERT 200
GAZİANTEP 202

HOME FROM HOME 232 HOW TO LIGHT A BBQ 246 GLOSSARY 247 INDEX 248

DEPARTURE (Between London and Instanbul)

It's book two and I'm on a flight to Istanbul. Yeah, I've been to Istanbul before with the boys and done all the tourist shit: fed the seagulls *kağıt helva* on the Kadıköy ferry, dodged the shoe shiners and their scams in Taksim Square, eaten in the overpriced tourist traps under the Eminönü Bridge, seen the beautiful architecture of the Blue Mosque and almost got beaten up by an old, drunk Turkish guy. But this is the first leg of my solo Türkiye trip. With Istanbul being a city of twenty million people, there's gotta be plenty of delicious food to eat out here. Normally, when traveling, my rule of thumb is to stay away from the bigger cities. I've eaten shit pasta in Rome, questionable steak tartare in Paris, and expensive fries in Belgium. Good fries to be fair—but I'm still pretty sure I got ripped off.

As a north Cypriot, I grew up eating Turkish food, however have always felt a disassociation with the "motherland." As Cyprus isn't recognized by the EU, the only memories that I have of mainland Türkiye are landing there for layovers during the 1990s. To get to Cyprus, we would have to stop either in Istanbul, Antalya or Izmir. Here the prim-and-proper speakers would exit the flight, and on would hop the darker-skinned, slang-speaking Cypriots. We would get to look at Türkiye out of the window, trying to rub away the condensation that had developed through the double glazing. It would usually be dark so, to me, Türkiye was always just a yellow security-lit airport. That was back when you could smoke cigarettes on planes—long before speedy boarding and sushi restaurants had a heavy airport presence, and there were terribly slow tablets provided as onboard entertainment. The only tablets you actually need for flying are Valium. I popped one 40 minutes ago and I feel warm, fuzzy and excited. I always get an extra leg room seat. Flying bugs me out, man. I hate feeling like no one wants to sit next to me—because although I take up space, I'm a good stranger to sit next to.

No one is sitting next to me on the outbound flight. It's just me, my diazepam and the airplane food. I don't actually mind plane food, you know. It's not actually as shit as people make it out to be.

Today's gourmet airline lunch is a pretty small chicken breast, braised in tomato, onion and garlic, topped with a big spliff's worth of oregano. Dry as hell, but has flavor. It's served with, what I can only describe as, a sad zucchini and a single roasted tomato. I remember Heston Blumenthal saying something about altitude changing your taste buds, so I always hit airplane food heavy with the salt. To be fair, with what I paid for the ticket, I'm surprised what I'm getting is even remotely edible.

I flick through the world's slowest entertainment system, knowing that I'm only looking for *The Office*. I hate trying to find things to watch; at home I'll flick through Netflix for 30 minutes, decide on something I know that I'm not really gonna have any interest in, then look at my phone while I eat candy in bed. Anyway, I decide to stick on *John Wick*. I've seen the first few—they're easy to watch—you don't really need to know who's who, or what the plot is. Keanu Reeves basically goes around bodying people the entire time; pushing his jacket above his chin to protect himself from enemies with a bad aim. My tiny airline headphones blast tin-like gunshots deep down my ear canal, reminiscent of DVD days. Me and John Wick actually have a lot in common: Tall? Check. Dark? Check. Handsome? Check.

To be completely honest, before this year, I didn't ever really consider writing a book about Turkish food. I grew up as a half-English, half-Turkish-Cypriot kid, and the family recipes that I wrote in book one felt complete. I didn't cover Cypriot cuisine in its entirety, but many of the meals championed in the Semay household were written and printed for everyone to consume. It felt good to fly the Turkish-Cypriot flag—I was able to speak about its history on TV in the press campaign for the book. Introducing northern Cyprus, a country of only 330,000 people, to a new audience was a proud moment for me, especially being the son of a war prisoner. Belligerent, work-driven and apprehensive of taking any risks: my dad, Kamil, is a calculated man. He's intelligent, although some of his ideologies may be narrow. He's never been deemed as booksmart, but he's a man of

street-sense (village streets, not the city ones I used to mess around on). He's a good judge of character and knows when someone's on bullshit. He's polite and kind, at times, but can change at the flick of a switch. You may be wondering why you're reading about Kamil in the introduction to my cookbook. Well, without Kamil, I wouldn't be here—nor would I be Turkish.

Kamil is the first link in the chain of me growing up Turkish; the culture-clash that I feel that my childhood was. We were always fed, watered and warm, but it wasn't always sunny in Edmonton, North London. My mom and dad didn't always see eye-to-eye and, of course, kids aren't dumb. They call kids "little sponges," soaking up information. But life isn't as easy as squeeze, rinse and repeat. Your experiences and memories as a child are the marinade for your life as an adult. Kamil would do anything for me as a kid, although I'm definitely his most problematic child. If I needed him, he was there in a heartbeat. There were no lengths that Kamil wouldn't go to make sure we were safe. I remember a time that he made a man wind down his window to punch him in the face after he cut us off in traffic. It sounds fun, having a dad who's hard as nails. But sometimes I just wanted a dad who would come home on time to take me to a mate's birthday at the sports complex in Finchley—not one who dragged me to a Turkish social café where I'd listen to him go on about how he made 6ft+ sons.

In all honesty, I neglected my Turkish side when I saw the dramas between my mom and dad. Mom would openly throw jabs at Dad when he wasn't at home, but it was almost subconsciously that I completely shut the door on the Turkish aspects of my life. Alev, my sister, is fluent in Turkish. My brother, Arif, is a walking Cyprus flag. And I was a mama's boy. My mom has always been an English rose to me, and I guess that leaves Kamil as the thorn. I started to associate anything Turkish with the negative emotions I felt towards Kamil. Talking to aunties and uncles on the phone to make my dad happy? No way. Going to Cyprus on vacation? I'm alright, thanks. Talking in Turkish to anyone? I'm good. Slowly but surely, the identity crisis began.

I was a rebellious child, kicking up a fuss at school and back-talking my parents. But, really, I was rebelling against my own identity. I associated anything to do with my dad with the same feelings. It's why I stayed away from Cyprus, it's why I didn't want to go to Turkish school, it's why I didn't identify myself with the little sub-pockets of international kids at school. I'm a London boy through-and-through; the culture, the lifestyle, the aesthetic. It's all London for me: 95s, Academik tracksuits and Lot 29 t-shirts. I'm that kind of London. 99 pence-3-wings-and-chips-London. 40 pence-bus-fare-London. Panda-pops-and-penny-sweets-London. It's not easy being of a mixed background and trying to figure out where you sit in the world of social brackets of multicultural Britain. On the outside, I don't look British and I have a foreign name. Sometimes I feel like people are almost surprised when they get to know me. They expect me to be a weed-smoking grime-head with no understanding of anything outside of that space. So where the fuck do I fit in? My Turkish is good enough now to hold a short chit-chat convo or order food, and my English vocabulary is refined enough to surprise people. I'm a foreigner in North London and a foreigner in Cyprus. So, where the fuck is home? Where is the soil I can pick up in a field and be like, "Aahhh, the Motherland"?

Looking back on it now, I'm a little embarrassed: taking on second-hand smoke and allowing it to consume me enough that I was willing to completely wipe away my Turkish side. I dissociated from my roots, culture and, most importantly, family. Pulling away from my Turkish side has come up a few times in therapy and, the more I talk about it, the more I can make sense of it. Rebellion is pretty much a self-sabotage mission—we all have underlying issues that we don't wanna deal with, and in return it's just easier to be a little prick. At the time, we don't know why we are behaving a certain way, but then: BAM—you're 32 and the penny drops.

I've never traveled alone before—never been backpacking, never done any of that Thailand-elephant pants stuff. I've had enlightening experiences at home. I've been to New York, Spain, France, Sri Lanka, Italy—and multiple trips to Cyprus—all with other people. Come to think of it, until now, I've never spent any real time on my own. Never lived alone, I've always had someone there. In the last three years since getting my dalmatian, Denzil, I've had a constant second shadow that follows me and pisses in the backyard. I don't mind silence—I talk to myself in my head. I'm enjoying doing that more often, now that I do live TV appearances and have to be switched on at all times.

I am exactly what you see on TV and YouTube. My mission isn't to be famous and I'm not even that much of a celebrator. I don't really celebrate wins or take the time to acknowledge my achievements. Being on TV or getting paid to plug a piece of cooking apparatus aren't all it for me. Getting to Head Chef, not becoming a drug dealer, never doing blow—*those* are all things to be celebrated in my little world of North London: not falling victim to the system, the cycle of negativity that comes with the lower working-class streets. Success for me isn't measured by number of followers, brands I'm associated with or what morning TV show I'm cooking on. Come to think of it, I don't really know what success actually looks like. What are you doing right now and for what? Whether it be saving for a house, paying off a car, being surrounded by people who will be there 'til the end; success is a personal journey.

I'm a firm believer that you shouldn't measure anyone else's shit against your own. Unfortunately, that's become a lot harder over the years and the only thing to blame for it is social media. The repetitive chip-chop cooking videos, "Let's make all the soups from around the world," and my most hated of them all: GRWM. Why have I wasted an hour of my life watching someone I'll never meet getting fucking ready?! The person you think has it all is very much still battling the same shit you're battling. Yeah, they might have a little more money in their pockets and have ugly *Love Island* sofas in their living rooms, but their journey should mean fuck all to you. I don't know if I'll ever sit back one day in a silk morning robe, smoking a cigarette, stroking multiple dogs in front of a crackling fireplace. Right now, I'm just gonna keep it moving. OK, the freebies are great, but I just wanna be known as that guy who makes food easy, who bridges the gap between suits and tracksuits and breaks the middle-class boundary that food carries.

There isn't really any of that in Türkiye, classism in food—apart from Salt Bae who is pretty much the only celebrity of the food scene there. Locals ain't really fucking with him though. No one's like, "I'm sick of *fasulye*. Let me eat a steak covered in gold that costs four times my wages for the week." That type of restaurant is aimed at people who want to be famous and never will be. They're people who want to be seen and enjoy a lifestyle that's only achievable once every quarter. The real food in Türkiye is affordable and doesn't have any social boundaries. It doesn't matter if you're in a suit, or if your hands are covered in oil from fixing Fiat taxis all day: they believe everyone deserves good food.

Let me just make this clear, this is a book on Turkish food through *my* lens. This isn't a complete history of Turkish politics or social injustice. It's just food. Throughout my trip, I'm gonna steer away from anywhere that is a "destination" restaurant. By that, I mean places where people enjoy the ambience and taking pictures of their food, instead of enjoying that valuable moment when a dish is presented to you. They're usually places where chefs are going with the novo-cuisine approach. It's not my style, it's not food that I'm excited about, and it doesn't represent the vast landscape and history of Turkish food. I reckon I feel like that due to many years working in the London-Italian restaurant circuit throughout my career. It was at Fifteen and Rotorino that I learned how simple food can be executed with respect; whether it be an artichoke or a piece of meat.

If you ever catch me in a restaurant, I have a thing for smelling food. When a dish is presented to me, I often pick it up and give it a quick whiff—not to see if it's bad or anything—but because food is sensory and not solely visual. The sounds are just as important: pasta clapping against a pan before

VOILE POUR
RENTRER HAGIA SOPHIA
EN VENTE ICI
DE QUALITE ET BON PRIX
Добро
Внимание!!!
Вход в Айя София
только в платке
SU_10 T.L
AYRAN_10 T.L
M.SUYU_10 T.L
SU_10 T.L
AYRAN_10 T.L
M.SUYU_10 T.L

aysan

it's plated, screaming hot bread fresh from the wood oven—desperate for someone to rip it open so it can relax. Obviously then there's taste—which is perfectly summarized in that scene from *Ratatouille*. Remy, the crafty little French rat, explains how food tastes to him through vibrant flecks of neon fireworks. He explains how flavor profiles work individually and when combined. To be honest with you, that's how food works for me, too. I'm just a little half-Turkish rat.

Eating on your own, in silence, is a good thing to do once in a while. Food is a social thing, however, taking time once in a while to be fully invested in a bowl of food with no interruptions is important. Food's romantic, on the cusp of being sexual. Meals that you eat in silence are not the type of ones you quickly forget about. So I'm on my own, heading to Türkiye. I know heading on a solo food research trip is gonna be different. I'm not planning to go to beaches or see things like I normally would on a vacation; I'm heading straight to the places in Türkiye that I've been told by cab drivers in the UK to visit.

We touch down and it feels like I've been in a time machine for the last ninety minutes; what with the 1980's décor and strong yellow lighting. Not only have I landed in the 1980s, but my bag hasn't been regurgitated by baggage claim yet. The diazepam I took ten hours ago has worn off and I'm not panicking, but I'm a little like "What the fuck am I even doing here?". That's just nerves, though. I don't know about you, but the narrator in my head is a huge pessimist that's constantly playing devil's advocate. I tell my brain to pipe down and go on the hunt for my suitcase. Turns out it had to go through an extra search because I was the only person on the flight whose journey started abroad. There it is: final confirmation that I'm gonna be fully alone for the foreseeable.

01

THE BASICS

BEYOGLU (Istanbul, Northern Türkiye)

Istanbul is a major city in Türkiye, but not the capital, despite often being mistaken for it—much like people get confused with the Canberra/Sydney situation in Australia. Türkiye's actual capital is Ankara, in the central region. Istanbul straddles Europe and Asia across the Bosphorus Strait. Its Old City reflects the cultural influences of the many empires that once ruled here: in the Sultanahmet district there's an open-air, Roman-era Hippodrome once used for chariot races, Egyptian obelisks remain, and the iconic Byzantine Hagia Sofia features a soaring 6th-century dome with rare Christian mosaics.

I touch down here with more important things on my mind: starving, ears hurting from the little tin-can plane headphones, fingers hurting from playing my Nintendo switch, back tight and legs swollen from the cabin pressure. It's midnight and all the shit airport restaurants are closed. I jump in a seven-seater taxi (because that's the way to do it in Istanbul), light up a cigarette and send the obligatory "I'm here and safe" text messages back home. It's a dark, warm night. The cab man bombs down the motorway, passing high-rise after high-rise, as the meter moves into the thousands, which looks a lot but is really only equal to thirty bucks.

I'm happy to be here but a little nervous, I'm not going to lie. Aside from booking an apartment in Beyoglu for the next three weeks, in true Hasan fashion, I've done no research. I blew my advance payment for the book about eight months before we'd even decided what book two was going to be, which has eaten into my budget, affecting the way I'm doing this trip—but ultimately will make it more authentic. The "move" to Istanbul (I call it a move because it's not actually a vacation at this point, it's a solo food mission that I'm being paid to do, so technically that makes it work) came around quickly. I got paid from another gig on Monday and booked my ticket to arrive in Istanbul 48 hours later. A lot of my life is like that. Who's actually got the time to book things in advance and have a planner? It's not the way I'm built.

Some would argue that I don't get anything done the way I work, but the older I get, the more I wanna throw myself in the deep end and make shit happen from a spark of spontaneity. Some of the biggest gigs I've done, I purposely haven't prepped for until I'm in a cab; making notes on the way. I don't want time to dwell or overthink what I'm going to say, which takes the organic feel out of things. The first time I did *Saturday Kitchen*, I was naturally nervous, with a dry mouth, a foggy brain and constantly needing to pee—but I found I could quickly relax into TV presenting. While, physically, I'm often the tallest in a room, I retain the ability to blend into most situations. This doesn't come from a place of arrogance—I'm basically trying to say that even with under-planning, you can still make shit happen. It's just a different approach.

I get to my apartment at 2am. I open up all the windows and stand there in silence for a bit on the balcony. The road is filled with homeless people, who have quite obvious struggles with drink and drug addictions. The apartment building sits on a busy main road, which feels a little like living on the North Circular back in London. For some, the noise and grit could come across as intimidating but, to me, kinda feels like home. I'm used to the lifestyle that goes with living below the bread line.

I wander down the high road—I know it's 3am, but what's the worst that's gonna happen? After five minutes of walking, I find a little workman's *lokanta* (diner) decked out in bright white LED tube lighting that's serving loads of steaming Turkish dishes in a canteen-style service counter. Rows of men sit in straight lines, all looking up towards the TV as the glare bounces off the glazed wooden paneling on the walls. I order roasted eggplant stuffed with ground meat, big roasted wedges of oddly cut potatoes, salad, and a whole loaf of bread. I walk the food back to the apartment and eat while channel hopping between late-night Turkish TV shows.

The following morning, the sun is beaming in through the curtains. It's a weird feeling waking up without a 100 lb (45 kg) Dalmatian next to me. It isn't until midday that I notice I haven't said anything out loud and am already settling into having conversations in my head. When I'm home alone, it's usually with the dog, so I'm not actually by myself. I talk to Denzil quite often; whether it be: "Stop doing that" or "You alright, my boy?". There's always noise—but the silence of my first morning is something I immediately notice. Scoping out the local shop is one of the first things I want to do, so that I know where I can buy cigarettes. Growing up in London, I've always had the convenience of having a late-hours corner store in walking distance to buy whatever I need at whatever time. Trust me, no one has seen you as vulnerable or beat up as your local shopkeeper.

After I've picked up cigarettes and had my first verbal conversation of the day with the shopkeeper, I wander around the streets from Beyoglu to the Sultan Ahmet mosque, which takes about an hour. This blue mosque is a central location I recognize and one that I can use to get my bearings. As I approach, pillars beam high into the heavens, and the multiple lidded domes blend into the sunny sky. Until now, I've never been in a mosque before; never been the religious type nor was it a thing in my household. But, I must say, there's a certain feeling walking in here: a holy serenity about it. Inside it's cool in temperature because of all the marble. A blue and red repeated pattern of Islamic filigree stretches from the floor to the ceilings as men pray in tandem, mirroring one another. I understand the general belief practices of Islam, but there is an unspoken brotherhood and sisterhood behind faith here in Türkiye. It's a positive influence on society—not only the happiness of bringing people together, but encouraging sacred time to yourself to pray, reflect or just be grateful. I decide I want to check out the Hagia Sofia and the Sultan Ahmet mosques that are also here in Istanbul, and said to be almost football stadium size in stature.

Next to the closed market, I pick up a döner kebab from Dönerci Şahin Usta. In the UK and Europe, döner are typically associated with drunk nights out and unhealthy food, but it's the first thing I think of when I think of Istanbul. I line up for 45 minutes to collect my order, but honestly it's the best döner I've eaten to date: just the right amount of fatness in the meat, warm and pillowy bread, a wetness from tomatoes, sharp and punchy sliced onions, finished with pul biber, folded in half like a quesadilla and served with a smile. I eat five in total over the next three weeks in Istanbul, each time getting a little more meat than before as a reward for returning and having a chat with the staff there. Five meat-juice-stained t-shirts later, I'd had my fix.

SERVES 4

Rice is a huge part of Turkish cuisine; it's one of the three most important carbs in a Turkish household, along with bread and potatoes, and sometimes all are served at once. The fragrance of just-cooked basmati reminds me of bread and yogurt, as commonly these would all be served together for dinner. Turks tend to use baldo rice, which is a short, stubby grain that grows native to Türkiye, but I find that basmati is the easiest to cook and, for me, is the best tasting.

It's hard to write a rice recipe when it has been passed down generationally; my mom was taught by Kamil's mom, who would have been taught by her mom and so on. I still use their fingertip method (see below) when cooking rice. Mom taught me to cook rice like this long before I was a chef, and it's how I'll teach my kids, too. Don't let me catch you boiling rice, draining it and then steaming it. There's one way to tell who can cook well in professional kitchens—test that new chef who's spent all of their time cooking Michelin food by cooking rice.

ŞEHRİYELİ PİLAV Everyday rice

1 mug of basmati rice
8 tbsp (115 g) butter
splash of olive oil
2½ oz (70 g) crushed vermicelli
enough water or stock to cover your rice
sea salt

Measure out the rice—I don't ever deal in half measures when it comes to rice as I turn any leftovers into fried rice or a rice salad the next day. It's very important that you rinse your rice before cooking, otherwise it'll be too starchy and won't separate into individual grains. Also, the starch affects the flavor. Rice is often seen as a bulker and a carrier of flavor but that doesn't mean it can't be delicious. I wash my rice in a sieve over a bowl so that the water can pass through freely. Let the water run and you'll see how murky it is. Give the rice a little stir with your hand in a claw shape, don't squeeze it or be rough with it, otherwise you'll break the grains. Leave the water to run for at least 5 minutes until it runs clear.

Once the water is clean, cover the rice in fresh water, there isn't a measurement here, just cover it. Let the rice soak for at least 30 minutes.

About 5 minutes before the rice is done soaking, set a pot over medium heat, preferably one with a heavy base for better heat distribution. Add 3½ tablespoons of the butter with a splash of olive oil to stop the butter from burning. Once the butter has melted, add the vermicelli. Toast for a good 5 minutes until it's a deep brown color and the butter starts to smell like Werther's Originals.

Drain the rice and add it to the pot. Cook the rice until any moisture has evaporated. You'll notice a difference in sound—when the rice first goes in it'll sound like flowing water, when that starts to sound like a frying hiss, it's time to add salt and liquid. Season the rice generously. In terms of liquid, you can go for stock or water. (Side note: filtered or bottled water makes better rice than tap. Try it.) Add enough liquid so your fingertip under the waterline is touching the

rice and the liquid is level with the first crease in your index finger. When you're happy with the water level, taste the liquid to see if it's seasoned enough. Cover the pot with a lid and bring it to a boil.

Once the rice is boiling, add the remaining butter, then move the pot to your smallest burner over the lowest heat. Continue to cook the rice for 10 minutes. Please set a timer. Once the timer is done, turn off the heat, remove the lid, stick a clean, dry tea towel over the rice, put the lid back on and let it sit for at least 15 minutes or up until you are ready to eat. The sign of perfect basmati is that when you lift the lid, the grains of rice should be pointing up at you. That's your little rice audience thanking you for the good job you've done.

Iç pılav is normally a side dish to roast meats but is also used as a stuffing. My Nene used to make this back in the day, but she would put livers in. I can't stand liver, so have omitted. It's a dish typically served at family gatherings like weddings, birthdays or funerals.

IÇ PILAV Turkish rice with nuts and raisins

1 mug of baldo rice
¾ cup (100 g) almonds
¾ cup (100 g) pine nuts
2 tbsp olive oil
2 cups (300 g) roughly diced onions
8 tbsp (120 g) butter
1 cinnamon stick
1 tbsp ground allspice
2 cups (475 ml) vegetable stock
⅔ cup (100 g) raisins
sea salt and pepper

Please always wash your rice—it breaks my heart when you don't. Wash your rice thoroughly until the water runs completely clear. Washing away the starch helps make rice perfectly fluffy. Soak the clean rice in fresh water for 30 minutes while you get on with making the base.

In a dry pan over medium heat, toast the almonds until they're nice and brown. We don't want any dark or burnt spots, just a nice, even caramel color, which will take 5–8 minutes. Once the almonds are toasted, remove them from the pan and toast the pine nuts in the same way. With the pan already hot, the pine nuts will need less than half the cooking time. Remove the nuts from the pan and set aside.

In the same frying pan, warm the olive oil over medium heat and cook the onions. Add a big pinch of salt and leave them for about 15 minutes until they are soft, sweet and translucent.

In a medium saucepan, melt the butter until it starts to foam. Add the cooked onions, toasted nuts, cinnamon stick and allspice. Allow the spices to gently warm in the butter for a couple minutes until they are aromatic. We don't want to burn anything at this stage; take care with cooking the base—don't rush it.

Add the raisins and washed rice to the spiced butter. Stir everything together and let it fry for a couple of minutes, stirring occasionally to make sure the rice doesn't stick. Add the stock, then season with salt and a good few cracks of pepper. Give the rice one final stir, then leave to cook over medium heat until the stock comes to a boil.

Once the stock has reached a rolling boil, turn the heat to low and allow to cook, uncovered, until all the liquid has evaporated. When all the stock has been absorbed by the rice, remove the saucepan from the heat and cover with a clean, dry tea towel. Top with the saucepan lid and leave the rice to steam for at least 15 minutes.

Run a fork through the rice so that it's nice and fluffy when you're ready to serve it.

MAKES 10 SHEETS

Filo is believed to have originated in Türkiye. Nowadays, many variations exist as it has passed through different cultures over many generations. I asked questions while in Gaziantep, got some good intel and, with the help of a few nights of watching how-to videos on YouTube, finally got there. This pastry can be used for sweet or savory recipes. It's a little tricky to get the hang of, so don't worry if it's not perfect. All we're looking for is light and crispy.

YUFKA Filo pastry

4¼ cups (510 g) all-purpose flour, plus extra for dusting
1¾ cups (410 g) water
7 tbsp (100 g) butter
1 tbsp vegetable oil

This is a lot easier if you have a stand mixer as the dough is pretty wet; if not, just be patient with it, it will come together. Add the flour and water to a mixer and mix on a medium setting for about 10 minutes; same if you're doing it by hand. Cover the dough in a bowl and let it rest for at least 30 minutes. This part is important because mixing creates heat and if the dough is too warm it won't stretch but will tear instead.

Once the dough has rested, roll into a sausage on a floured work surface. Split the dough into 10 equal pieces and shape them into balls.

On a heavily floured work surface, press the balls to flatten and give them a once over with a rolling pin. Don't make them too thin, otherwise they'll stretch when you pick them up. I can't tell you how many times I stretched the filo for it to break before swearing in Turkish and throwing it in the trash. So be patient, not only with the dough but with yourself. This shit is done by specialists in Türkiye, so give yourself a pat on the back for attempting it. Roll the dough balls into CD-sized circles.

Melt the butter and add the oil. We're gonna use this mixture to stop the dough sticking, and aid ability to stretch it out. Using a pastry brush, coat a plate with the butter mixture. Stack the dough circles on the plate, making sure you coat each layer in between with a generous brush of the mixture. Wrap the stack of dough in plastic wrap and rest at room temperature for 35 minutes. Keep the rest of the butter mixture but don't refrigerate, as the butter will harden.

Now, make as much space as possible; it's time to stretch. Gently pick up a circle of dough and lay on the work surface. Using both hands, lift up the rim and gently pull the dough while wafting to create air underneath. Do this all the way round until the dough has tripled in size. It'll be almost translucent. The rim of the dough will be a lot thicker than the middle, so trim it away. That's the basic technique for stretching filo. Repeat with the remaining dough circles.

I've got two recipes on pages 170 and 218 that you can make using this filo. If you're making the dough in advance, wrap in plastic and store in the fridge (before stretching and coating with the remaining butter).

MAKES 2¼ LB (1 KG)

I went to Trabzon knowing that the food would be different. It's on the Black Sea so there's loads of seafood, but as it's only down the road from the Turkish highlands there's also a huge cheese and butter presence in the cuisine. The local climate influences the vegetation, with pastures and forests covering most of the land. The milk produced by cows grazing in these meadows, which significantly impacts the quality of the butter, is distinctively rich in yellow color. There's nothing like homemade butter and it's very simple to make. I really enjoy taking something we take for granted and understanding how it's made and then bragging about it. It's a chef thing, I guess.

TEREYAĞI Homemade butter

7½ cups (1.8 liters) heavy cream, cold
sea salt (optional)

You're gonna need a stand mixer for this. If you're using a mixer with a metal bowl, stick the whisk and the bowl in the freezer about 30 minutes before you start. The friction and how long the mixer will be going for will generate heat and we don't want our cream to heat up. Also, make sure the cream is cold, like straight from the fridge, no messing around. Set up the mixer with the cold whisk and mixing bowl, pour in the cream and turn the mixer on. Don't go full whack straight away or you'll end up with cream all over your kitchen. Gradually build up the speed just to make sure there's no spillage. Once you know it's safe, crank it to high and let the mixer do its thing—the cream will start to thicken and become stiff. Make sure you scrape the bowl down so that all the cream is being used.

Once the cream has got to its thickest point, it will slowly start to split, meaning that the cream will look a bit lumpy and curdled. Stop the mixer, scrape everything back down into the bowl and let it keep mixing. It'll get to a point where the butter will separate, leaving liquid behind and butter on the top. The liquid is buttermilk and, if you really wanted to, you could keep it for salad dressings or marinades, but there aren't really any recipes in this book that call for it so you can do what I did and toss it. Once you've got rid of the buttermilk, let the butter keep mixing at half-power for a couple of minutes. This is just to get any more buttermilk out, if there's any left. When there's no more liquid coming out, take the butter out of the mixer and set it to one side.

In order for the butter not to turn rancid quickly, you need to wash it and squeeze out any remaining moisture. Fill a large mixing bowl with iced water and break the butter into four pieces—it doesn't matter if they're equal or not. Squeeze the butter under the water aggressively between your fingers, squelching any liquid out. I gave each block about 8 squeezes in the water, changed the water and repeated again. After that, your butter is pretty much good to go. It's up to you if you want to season it or not but I like mine packed with salt. Dry off any excess water using a clean kitchen cloth, stick it in a

bowl and give it 2 big grinds of salt. I shaped mine into logs, wrapped them in parchment paper and left them in the fridge. If you've squeezed out all the buttermilk properly, the butter will keep in the fridge for about 3 weeks. Honestly, it sounds like a lot of work but it really isn't.

EF GF

MAKES 6 QUARTS (6 LITERS)

The more I traveled around Türkiye, the more I noticed that, like the Italians and the French, the Turks rely on a good stock to bring depth to soups, meatiness to rice, or a roundness to a stewed kebap. This is my version of an entry-level chicken stock—in a professional kitchen this would be called a blonde chicken stock—sticky and gelatinous from using only chicken wings, but light in feel and in flavor. I'm a strong believer in using stock wherever you can use water. It's one of the fundamental things we learn as chefs. In a working kitchen there's always a huge pot with offcuts of vegetables and trimmings from meat prep bubbling away to look after everyone.

TAVUK SUYU Chicken stock

6 lb 8 oz (3 kg) chicken wings, plus any free chicken bones your butcher will give you
2 leeks, washed and split down the middle
1 bunch of celery, washed
2 large white onions, quartered
2 carrots, peeled
¼ bunch of thyme
4 bay leaves
sea salt, to taste

You're gonna need a really big pot for this. You need a pot between the 16–22 quart (16–22 liter) mark. If you don't have one, go and buy one. Every household needs one. Add the chicken wings to your stock pot and cover them completely in water. Stick the pot over the highest heat and bring to a boil. We're doing this to clean off our wings—you'll see how much gunk and foam rises to the rim, so please don't skip this part. You can't rush stock.

Discard the murky water and rinse the wings under cold water. Clean out the stock pot, since any little impurities will cause the stock to get cloudy. Although that's not so bad when using stocks for soups, it's best to do things properly.

There are no awards here for how you chop your veg, just make sure there's no skin on your onions (fine for a brown stock, not for a blonde). Stick the rinsed wings back into the stock pot along with all the chopped veg and the herbs. Fill the pot with water, leaving a 1 inch (2.5 cm) gap at the top. Bring to a boil, then drop the heat to a gentle simmer. The stock will still bring up gunky foam and fat on top, so skim that away with a ladle. Let the stock simmer, uncovered, for at least 2 hours. At no point should it boil again—you want soft, gentle blips.

Once the stock has simmered for 2 hours, strain it using a sieve to get rid of all the meat and vegetables. Using the same ladle, squash the chicken bones while they're still in the sieve to remove any excess moisture.

Strain the stock a second time using a finer sieve. If you went out to buy a stock pot for this recipe, chances are you won't have a fine sieve either. Instead you can place a clean kitchen cloth, pair of tights with a low denier, or piece of cheesecloth over the sieve you are using and pour the liquid through—you'll see why once you've done it. Season lightly.

Use the stock straight away or allow it to cool to room temperature before refrigerating. Store in the fridge for up to 3 days, or freeze for up to 3 months in a sealed airtight container.

MAKES TWO 5-QUART (5-LITER) CONTAINERS

Soups are the quickest and cheapest food in Türkiye. You'll often go to a soup shop and most made to order are flavored stocks that cook quickly. When I was in Adana, I had Beyran soup for the first time, an aggressive-looking, bright red soup with cooked rice, lamb, a heaped tablespoon of pul biber and butter. All the ingredients are put into a copper dish on a concentrated gas burner that roars. Two big ladles of meat stock bring the soup together and the spice sits on top. Simply delicious, which would be nothing without a good stock.

Consider this a master stock or base to most dishes. Why use regular old water when you can use flavored water for body? If you make any of the meat recipes in this book (see pages 156–199), you can use the bones, like the rib meat for the köfte recipes on pages 167 and 196. I always keep a bag of bones in the freezer. Making stock sounds like a time-consuming task, but you don't have to do much apart from cover and put up with the smell while it cooks.

ET SUYU Meat stock

- 2 lb 10 oz (1.2 kg) chicken wings
- 2 lb 10 oz (1.2 kg) beef or lamb bones
- 1 bunch of celery
- 4 carrots
- 3 onions
- 1 fennel bulb

Preheat the oven to 400°F (200°C).

Start by roasting the chicken wings and meat bones for 45 minutes–1 hour, until golden. Normally, when making a "brown stock" in a professional kitchen, you'd roast all the vegetables with tomato paste, hard herbs and a glug of red wine. That's great for making pan sauces and reductions, but we want this stock to be light and clean in flavor for use as a base.

Roughly cut all your veg—including any odds and ends like the skins or tops that you'd normally throw on the compost heap. Add your cut veg and browned bones to a stock pot and cover with water. The rule of thumb is that you should be able to push down the ingredients and have the water line come up to your wrist. This means there's enough liquid to absorb the flavors but won't reduce.

Bring to a boil. Depending on what meat bones you're using, the level of fat in the water will change so skim off any foam that rises. Once boiling, drop the heat to medium and let the stock gently simmer for about 4 hours. We want to cook the ingredients slowly to draw out as much flavor. If you do this too fast, the meat and veg will break down too quickly and the stock will be murky.

After 4 hours, drain the stock using a sieve. If your sieve's a bit crappy, strain again through a clean kitchen cloth. The stock now needs to cool to room temperature within 1½ hours to ensure it doesn't turn into a bacteria farm. Pour into something with a wide surface area, such as a roasting pan.

Stock is freezable up to 3 months when stored in an airtight container. Otherwise, refrigerate for up to 3 days.

TURŞU Pickles

Turks are pickle-crazy; they're cheap, easy to make and go with everything, from a fermented black carrot juice with balık ekmek on the seafront at Eminönü, fiery pickled cayenne peppers served with a sandwich, or crunchy, sharp cabbage with lentil soup. I feel like there was a point in my career when every restaurant I worked in was serving them: pickling mustard seeds for steak recipes, lacto-fermenting carrots for some celebration-of-carrots dish or a sweet pickle for a dessert. I don't mess about with fancy stuff now though. It's mostly about the balance between vinegar, sugar and salt. A good pickle can bring a roundedness to a dish, sharpness to cut through fat, crunch to break textures, and acid to bring vibrancy and freshness.

I've always got a pickle of some sort in the fridge, from Korean kimchi to Polish kraut. I always feel like the cucumbers in Turkish pickles are a little shit. I think that's because they're more of a lacto-ferment, meaning they ferment with salt and don't have that sharp punctuation I want when eating something rich like crusty bread, proper butter, mustard or a cold cut. I know none of those things are very Turkish, but there are no rules here, this is literally for the love of pickles. It might take you an hour, but you can make a ton of pickles for next to no money and they're a great bang for your buck. If you wanna make loads, double the batch and get your ingredients from a restaurant wholesaler. There's often no tax on fresh produce and they might even give you a container that you can pickle in, too.

EF GF VG

MAKES ONE 1-GALLON (4-LITER) CONTAINER

SALATALIK TURŞUSU Cucumber pickles

12 Lebanese cucumbers
2¼ cups (550 ml) cups filtered water
10 tbsp superfine sugar
2¼ cups (550 ml) white wine vinegar
1 tbsp mustard seeds
1 bunch of dill, roughly chopped
sea salt

When you're buying cucumbers, try to buy the firmest and the straightest you can get your hands on. It will make your life a lot easier for this recipe. Wash the cucumbers and let them sit in the water while you get the pickle going.

Stick the water, sugar, vinegar and mustard seeds in a pot and bring to a boil. Remove from the heat and leave to cool.

Slice the top and bottom off the cucumbers and cut them vertically down the middle. Put the cucumbers in a bowl and give them 3 big grinds of salt. Let the cucumbers sit for a good 10 minutes to release their moisture.

Once the pickling liquid has cooled to room temperature, stick the cucumbers into sterilized jars or airtight plastic containers, add the dill and pour over the pickling liquid, then seal. The cucumbers don't need long—in 1½–3 hours they will have taken on enough flavor. But the longer they sit, the better they get. I let mine go untouched for about 2 weeks before enjoying. Once opened, store in the fridge for 3 weeks, making sure there's always enough liquid covering the cucumbers.

EF GF VG

MAKES ONE 1-GALLON (4-LITER) CONTAINER

KARIŞIK TURŞU Mixed pickles

- 1 head white cabbage
- 1 cauliflower
- 1 lb 5 oz (600 g) carrots, peeled
- 2 lb 4 oz (1 kg) baby cucumbers
- 6 garlic cloves
- 5¾ oz (160 g) long green chiles
- 6 small green chiles
- ½ bunch of flat-leaf parsley, chopped

FOR THE PICKLING LIQUID

- 2½ cups (600 ml) white wine vinegar
- 7½ cups (1.8 liters) water
- ½ cup (100 g) sea salt
- ⅔ cup (125 g) sugar

Cut the cabbage into 8 wedges, separate all the florets of the cauliflower, then slice the carrots and cucumbers into middle finger-width slices. I did mine with a crinkle cutter because I enjoy the aesthetic. Give all the veggies a good wash, then drain.

Mix all the ingredients for the pickling liquid until the salt and the sugar have dissolved. Pack the veggies into a big enough pickling container to contain them all, along with the garlic and the chiles. Pour over the pickling liquid to cover all the veg. Use the parsley to push down and stuff the veg into the liquid, making sure nothing is poking out the top, then put the lid on.

Every day, turn your pickle container upside down a couple times and burp them by opening the container so there isn't a huge gas build-up. Store upright in a cool place for about 2 weeks. Once opened, and as long as the pickles are covered in the liquid, they'll keep for at least 3 weeks in the fridge.

EF GF VG

MAKES ONE 1-GALLON (4-LITER) CONTAINER

ACI BIBER TURŞUSU Pickled chiles

- 7 oz (200 g) bullet chiles
- 7 oz (200 g) small green chiles

Wash all the chiles, leaving the stalks on, then dry them. Use the same pickling liquid as above and cover the chiles in the liquid.

Leave in a cool, dry place for at least a week, or 2 weeks for best results. As long as the pickles are covered in the liquid, they'll keep for at least 3 weeks , once opened, in the fridge.

THE NORTH FACE

02

MEZE

ISTANBUL (Northwestern Türkiye)

I promise myself on this trip I'm going to live like a local; taking no taxis and relying on understanding how the transportation system works. I rinse and repeat my walk and döner routine over the next three weeks in Istanbul, interceding trips on foot by catching buses and taking the tram—one night I even get on a boat out to the Bosphorus sea for no reason at all. I spend most evenings at home watching Turkish "where to eat?" videos on YouTube before building lists and finding them the next day. In a city like Istanbul, it's easy to get sucked into the tourist restaurant traps, or the shisha restaurants serving food, which are depressingly taking the city by storm. They're all decorated with the same tacky aesthetic: suede booths with gold trimmings, whiskey glasses of Coke, menus that look like comprehension homework. They're normally staffed by waiters and waitresses who are dolled up so much that they've developed a superiority complex. You can't cut cabbage badly and then charge me above and beyond just because you put it in some weird-shaped bowl with fresh pomegranate. I don't want a boob-shaped mound of bulgur pilavı. I have a strange feeling that a lot of this performative-style of restaurant is for people who have more money than sense. I steer so far away from these types of restaurants; each one cooking up the same thing as the next.

The only place I recommend you eat in Taksim Square, besides the dessert shops, is Zübeyir Ocakbaşı: a proper old-school, three-story kebap house. Each floor has its own mangal, and one chef dedicated to looking after it. When you walk in, you're hit with a smell of oregano blistering over butter-laced lavaş. A huge bronze mangal, embellished with hand-beaten patterns, sits center of a marble work-top, which diners can sit around on little stools. The magnificent heat from the grill fills the room, and sitting mangal-side means you're served almost like in a Japanese hibachi restaurant. The chef at the helm sits in an office chair; small dishes on hand to his right full of pul biber, kırmızı toz biber, salt and oregano. There's a filing cabinet being used for ingredients storage; I can see it's full of bread and seasoning trays. Chef sits reading order tickets while pulling skewers to the front of the grill in a philharmonic fashion: turning meat, seasoning bread, fire-roasting peppers and tomatoes simultaneously. The strong hum from the extraction fan sucks out the smell of hissing rendering fat, just enough to leave the smell of my childhood fresh in the air. Every so often, chef rings his bell and calls for service. He keeps his garnish in a tray underneath the mangal to stay warm.

A new customer walks in and, as they sit, are greeted with a bottle of cold water and some warm bread. The staff are attentive—not pushy—speaking good English. They won't try to bombard you with suggestions of eating lamb balls, upselling shit cuts as delicacies. Here I ate some of the best tavuk şiş (chicken shish) I've ever tasted; cooked hard and fast: meat soft from the use of yogurt, tangy marinade with pul biber and cumin, cooked until it's dangerously moist, on top of a lavaş to soak up all the juices. An accompaniment of fiery roasted peppers, dressed in a thick garlic yogurt, gives you the contrast you need between the heat and a refresher. Don't get takeout, please just sit in here and let the food you've ordered come in dribs and drabs as you observe from the best seat in the house.

There are an abundance of great restaurants in Istanbul—but to find them, you've got to look for where the locals are eating. If the restaurant you're looking at is on Tripadvisor, the mains are over $30 and there's some sort of Mediterranean sushi on the menu, then you need to quickly bolt. Instead, take a little stroll down to Kumkapı which is at the very bottom of the city. There's rows of restaurants along this strip selling freshly caught fish, as well as cushioned-seat spots to sit and listen to bands playing live music. Low tables with glass tops are armored with paper tablecloths and bright orange napkins to clean hungry hands ready for eating meze. The strip itself is dedicated to meze, fish and rakı. Rakı is a twice-distilled grape alcohol, flavored with aniseed. Think ouzo or sambuca, but with a higher alcohol content that's typically between 40% and 50% AVB (80 to 100 proof). It's not a drink that you shot before a night out; it's paid huge respect and the food at Kumkapı is specifically designed around drinking rakı as an accompaniment aperitif.

GREEN

EF GF V

SERVES 4

In early spring in Cyprus, beets are everywhere. While eating at my auntie's, I thought I'd play around with complimentary flavors that are common in Türkiye and Cyprus. Traditionally, I'd use a beyaz peynir which is fattier and smoother than feta—but I love feta just as much and it's easier for you guys to find. This is a really clean and simple meze, no fuss. Serve with plenty of bread.

PANCAR VE BEYAZ PEYNİR

Beet, feta and pistachios

1 lb 5 oz (600 g) raw beets
½ garlic clove
3 tbsp full-fat thick yogurt
1¾ oz (50 g) feta, frozen
2 tbsp pistachios, crushed
couple of mint leaves
sea salt and pepper

TO DRIZZLE
pomegranate molasses
olive oil

Give the beets a little rinse under the faucet just to make sure there's no dirt on them. Stick them in a pot and cover with cold water. Make sure the pot is big enough so the beets are fully submerged and have enough room to float without touching. Heavily season the water and bring to a boil.

Once boiling, drop the heat to medium. Simmer for about 40 minutes until they're soft enough to get a fork through with no resistance. Drain the beets while they're still hot and peel the skins under cold running water.
Let the beets come down to a cool enough temperature to work with.

Grate all but one of the beets on the biggest side of a box grater. Gather all the grated beets and give them a good squeeze over the sink to remove all excess moisture. If you don't do this, they'll bleed into the yogurt and the dish will look weird.

Grate in the garlic and season the grated beets well with salt and pepper. Give it all a good mix. Add the yogurt and taste. I usually season a little whenever I've put a new ingredient in, just to keep building flavor.

Dollop the mixture onto a plate and spread it out so it's even, then zigzag over pomegranate molasses and the oil.

Remember that beet we put aside? I want you to dice it into beautiful little cubes. Season that with oil and salt and pepper, then stick on top.

Microplane over the feta so it's soft and heaping. Scatter with the pistachios, add the torn mint leaves and you're good to go.

EF GF VG

SERVES 2

These onions were served with every kebap I ate in Adana, are really easy to make, and great with all meats. Some people add slices of tomato and pomegranate molasses for wetness and sweetness but I like bold punchy food, so I leave it as is.

SOĞAN SALATASI Adana onions

- 1 white onion
- small handful of flat-leaf parsley
- pinch of cumin seeds, toasted and crushed
- pinch of kırmızı toz biber (Turkish paprika)
- pinch of sea salt

It's not rocket science this one. Thinly slice the onion, using a mandoline if you're not good with a knife, but be careful—those things are death traps.

Run a knife over the parsley casually, nothing too small, and add to the onion.

Add the spices and salt and massage it all together. Serve.

EF GF VG

SERVES 4

Gaziantep is the place in Türkiye with the most celebrated heritage dishes that herald from the Ottoman Empire. It's the Basque, Lyon or Bologna of Türkiye. When I spoke to locals about where to eat in Gaziantep, everyone tipped their hats to Halil Usta for their "wet salad." It's a chopped salad, but the base is juice from ripe tomatoes. The name for this salad split hairs while shooting the book, but once everyone ate it they got it. It shall always be referred to as wet salad and nothing else. If you can, get ripe, in-season tomatoes from a farm; it'll make such a difference. A lot of the tomatoes in supermarkets are watery and flavorless with an unripe watermelon texture. Salads in Türkiye aren't chemically-washed leaves in a bag that you forget about in the back of the fridge. They're celebrated just as much as the main dish.

GAZIANTEP SALATA Wet salad

3 beefsteak tomatoes
2 stumpy cucumbers
3 light green Charleston salad peppers
10 cherry tomatoes
3 scallions
2 heads Little Gem lettuce
1 tsp dried mint
2 tbsp pomegranate molasses
1 tsp red wine vinegar
extra virgin olive oil, for drizzling
sea salt

Start off by grating the beefsteak tomatoes using a box grater. Season the grated tomatoes with a good couple of cracks of sea salt, stick it in a sieve or a piece of cheesecloth and allow it to drain into a bowl, reserving the liquid. The salt will allow the liquid to drain faster.

While the tomatoes drain, zebra-peel the cucumbers. This basically means peel a bit lengthways, then miss a bit until you're left with a striped cucumber. Slice the cucumbers down the middle lengthways and remove the seeds. I always take the seeds out of cucumbers as they're full of water and don't carry a lot of flavor. Quarter the cucumbers and chop them into little bite-sized chunks.

Cut the green salad peppers to the same size, removing any seeds. Do the same with the cherry tomatoes and the scallions. Slice the Little Gem lettuces down the middle and slice them as thinly as possible.

Add all the chopped ingredients to a bowl, pour over the drained tomato liquid, season generously with salt, then add the dried mint and pomegranate molasses. Stir in the vinegar and dress with a good drizzle of extra virgin olive oil. The salad will be wet, but it's a great place to dunk bread.

SERVES 4

This is another meze that's designed to be eaten while drinking rakı. Even though you'll always find it in shitty British kebap shops, it's a top-tier dish. It's a great thing to dip warm bread into. It doesn't usually have cheese in it, but the feta gives it a sourness—a little extra something to keep you dipping.

HAYDARİ "Hung" yogurt and walnuts

7 oz (200 g) feta
3 cups (700 g) full-fat thick yogurt, plus 2 tbsp
½ tbsp water
1 garlic clove, grated
¼ oz (10 g) dill, finely chopped, plus extra sprigs to serve
sea salt

FOR THE DILL OIL
½ oz (15 g) parsley
1 oz (25 g) dill
scant 1 cup (200 ml) sunflower oil

TO GARNISH
¼ cup (30 g) walnuts
pinch of pul biber
pinch of cumin seeds, toasted and crushed

Let's start with the whipped feta element. Add the feta, 2 tablespoons of yogurt, the water and a big grind of salt into a blender—preferably a Nutribullet or something powerful that's going to break the feta down. Whizz it all together into a smoothish purée. Be careful not to split the mixture; blending ingredients warms them and we're whipping 2 things with a high fat content together. So, as soon as it comes together, turn the blender off.

Add the feta "purée" to the remaining yogurt in a bowl. Season again with salt, then stir in the garlic and dill. You can leave the yogurt mixture to chill in the fridge for up to 3 days. But if you've got a little time—hang it: put the mixture either in a cheesecloth or a thin pair of tights with a low denier and hang from a height. You'll want to place a bowl underneath to catch any excess liquid, which can be discarded. I normally do this in the fridge as the temperature helps it to thicken, but if that's not possible, I sometimes hang it on a washing line in the backyard overnight if its chilly out.

Finely chop the walnuts for the garnish and season with a sprinkle of salt, the pul biber and cumin and mix. Set aside to use later on.

Next, let's make a little oil—like the Michelin guys do to make a dish look fancy enough for it to cost $25. Combine the parsley and dill with the oil. Using a high-powered blender or stick blender, blend until the herbs have fully broken down and the oil is bright green in color. Pour the oil into a small frying pan and heat over low heat; we want to bring the oil up to heat gradually. Once the oil starts to bubble around the edges, the color will begin to change.

Once you start to get bigger bubbles in the center of the oil and the kitchen smells grassy, remove the oil from the heat and strain through a clean kitchen cloth, over a sieve, into a bowl. Don't force the mixture through with a utensil, just let it drip through. Pushing it through will cause the oil to go brown, as you're catching the stuff we want to leave behind.

When the yogurt mixture has thickened, either in the fridge or by being hung, it's ready to plate. I serve haydari in a bowl, using the yogurt mixture as a base. Make a well in the center. Sprinkle the walnut mixture on top, plus a couple of spoonfuls of the flavored oil. Garnish with dill springs and serve with bread.

EF GF VG

SERVES 4

Traditionally, muhammara has breadcrumbs and tomato paste in it, but I think the breadcrumbs go too soft and the purée makes it taste a little cheap. Instead, I grill loads of peppers and bulk it out with walnuts. Muhammara is great on bread, with meats, or even a couple of fried eggs with breakfast. Make it—you'll love it. Promise.

MUHAMMARA Pepper and walnut dip

- 10 Corno di Toro red peppers
- 1 red chile
- 1¼ cups (150 g) walnuts
- 1 tbsp pul biber
- 1 tsp cumin seeds, toasted and crushed
- 1 tsp acı toz biber (hot Turkish paprika)
- 2 garlic cloves, grated
- 3 tbsp olive oil
- 1 tbsp pomegranate molasses

Start off by getting your BBQ lit (see "How to Light a BBQ" on page 246). Obviously, if you don't have a BBQ, you can do this in a hot oven—around 475°F (240°C)—following the rest of the process.

Over a 1 count (see "How to Light a BBQ" on page 246), char the peppers and your one lonely chile on the grill. This shouldn't be quick—a good, solid char will take about 20 minutes until the peppers are cooked. You want the skins to blister and blacken and the flesh to be soft to the touch.

Once all the peppers and the chile are cooked, stick them in a bowl and cover with plastic wrap, a clean, dry tea towel or a plate in order to trap the moisture. Steam the peppers and chile for about 10 minutes until the skins are soft and easy to remove. Leave to cool.

Once the peppers are cool enough to handle, pull off the stems and remove any seeds. Peel away the skins and discard. Don't worry about the peppers being whole or looking pretty; they're going in a blender.

Blend the peppers and the chile together by pulsing a few times, so they're more of a chunky salsa consistency than a purée. Transfer the sauce from the blender to a bowl.

In the same blender, pulse the walnuts into small pieces. Stir the walnuts into the pepper sauce, along with the spices and garlic. Finish by drizzling with the olive oil and pomegranate molasses, then serve.

SERVES 4

Nobody knows who invented rakı, with there being many forms from the Med, Balkans and Middle East. What we do know is that it's a drink created by the countries that were once ruled by the Ottoman Empire. The Turks often refer to it as *aslan sütü*, meaning "lions' milk," with the belief that the drink gives men a fierce power in their loins. This is a beautiful dish to dip some warm bread into while drinking rakı. The version I had of this in Istanbul was made with raw carrots, but I cook mine quickly to bring the sweetness out of them.

HAVUÇ TARATOR Carrot, yogurt and walnuts

- 3 tbsp olive oil, plus extra for drizzling
- 3 garlic cloves, crushed
- 6 cups (600 g) grated carrots
- 1 tsp cumin seeds
- ½ tsp fennel seeds
- 1 tsp coriander seeds
- 2 tbsp white sesame seeds
- 1 tsp black sesame seeds
- 1 tsp pul biber
- 1 tbsp sumac
- 4 tbsp full-fat thick yogurt
- ¼ cup (25 g) walnuts
- sea salt and pepper

Heat a large frying pan with the olive oil over a high heat. Once the oil is hot, throw in the garlic and let it cook for about 30 seconds just to start to flavor the oil. Add the carrots and stir-fry for about 4 minutes, seasoning with salt and pepper. You want the carrots to still be crunchy but just not totally raw. You're basically blanching the carrots in a frying pan with oil instead of boiling water. Once the carrots are cooked, cool them down fast on a plate.

For the spice mix, toast the cumin, fennel and coriander seeds until they're fragrant and a little brown. I find the best way to toast seeds is to start them in a cold, dry pan and slowly bring them up to temperature so they can release their natural oils. When the spices are toasted, stick them into a mortar and pestle and grind them while they're still hot. In the same pan, toast the sesame seeds until they look a little oily. Add all the sesame seeds to the ground seeds, along with the pul biber and sumac.

Mix the cooled carrots and yogurt together and season with salt to taste.

Stick the mixture on a plate or in a dish, zigzag over some olive oil for a pepperiness and a break in color. Crumble the walnuts over the top and sprinkle over a couple of good pinches of the spice mix.

You know that time during a BBQ when you're waiting for the coals to come down to the right temperature—just after you've spread them? Well, that's the ideal time to char up some vegetables and make a fiery little dip. I serve grilled meat on top of grilled ezme, almost using it as a resting tray. It's a proper mop-up sauce vibe. As a chef, I was taught to utilize my time properly and work smarter, not harder, so it makes sense to use a grill that's coming up to temperature. It's almost an opportunity to set the flow of your evening, or what us white-jacket-wearing pricks call service.

IZGARA EZME Grilled ezme

- 3 small cucumbers
- 4 scallions
- 4 small red peppers, deseeded
- 4 beefsteak tomatoes
- 5 sprigs of mint
- ¼ oz (10 g) parsley
- 5 tbsp olive oil
- 4 tbsp pomegranate molasses
- juice of ½ lemon
- sea salt

FOR GRILLING

- 3 small green Kenyan chiles
- 5 long dark green Turkish peppers
- 3 beefsteak tomatoes
- 4 shallots
- 6 scallions

Take all the ingredients for grilling and stick them on the grill, skins on. You want a solid 2 count on the grill (see "How to Light a BBQ" on page 246). Don't worry about seasoning them, we're looking to char them over fire and pick up that smoky flavor—they almost cook in their own juices.

The little chiles will cook first; the skins will turn black and they'll fill with steam. Once the steam starts to escape and release, remove them from the heat and set to one side. The same applies for the long peppers. The rest you want to grill until the skins are charred and they start to soften—this will take anywhere between 15–20 minutes.

Once all the veg are charred, stick them in the same bowl and cover with plastic wrap to retain their heat and keep them moist.

Finely dice the raw ingredients: the cucumbers, scallions, red peppers and beefsteak tomatoes. We want them all pretty uniform so that they add crunch and their own textures in equal measure.

Run a knife over the mint and parsley to roughly chop and add to the diced veg salad.

By now, your grilled bits should be cool enough to handle. Peel to remove their soft skins and roughly chop together, on the same board. Imagine that you're making a salsa, trying to keep things nice and small.

Mix the cooked ingredients with the raw salad ingredients. Add the olive oil, pomegranate molasses and the lemon juice to create a light dressing and generously season with salt before serving.

EF GF VG

SERVES 4

We all know it, we all love it—and if you don't, I don't trust you. I'm gonna give you three recipe variations for this one: a standard smooth, silky hummus, one made with red lentils and one version with a little salad on top like they serve in Istanbul.

HUMMUS Classic hummus

2¼ cups (400 g) dried chickpeas, soaked overnight
1 tsp baking soda
½ cup (120 ml) ice-cold water
4½ oz (120 g) ice
generous 1 cup (300 g) tahini
juice of ½ lemon
2 garlic cloves
sea salt

TO SERVE

½ tsp cumin seeds, toasted and crushed
½ tsp smoked paprika
heaped 1 cup toasted pine nuts (optional)

To start off, let's go about making a proper hummus: not cutting corners using canned chickpeas—I expect you to soak, cook and peel the chickpeas yourself. Add the chickpeas to a large pot and cover with double the amount of water. Sprinkle in the baking soda and bring to a boil. The baking soda is going to help soften the skins on our chickpeas and help to cook them quicker.

Once the chickpeas are boiling, the water will start to foam. At this point, drop the heat to medium and gently simmer. You can remove the scum from the top, but you don't have to as we're not using any of the cooking water. Cook the chickpeas for 40 minutes until the skins have softened and you can break a chickpea by pinching it between 2 fingers. Inside, it should be smooth. Drain the chickpeas and give them a quick wash with some cold water.

Now, I wouldn't ask you to do this if it wasn't beneficial, but I'm gonna need you to remove the skin from each chickpea. The easiest way to do this is to rinse them in a bowl, under a strong tap, gently rubbing them in between your fingers, being careful not to crush them.

Once all the skins are removed, add your naked chickpeas to a blender. Add the ice-cold water and whizz together until the chickpeas to start to break down. Pause to add half the ice, then blend until there are no lumps.

Add the tahini, lemon juice and 3 big grinds of salt. Blend again, slowly adding the remaining ice. The tahini will give our hummus a nice color and the ice will keep the mix cool while the blender works through it. We're looking for the tahini to emulsify and hold the mixture together, almost like a glue.

At this point, you should have a beautiful, silky, loose hummus. If at any point it becomes too loose, add a little more of tahini to thicken it again. I know this sounds like a lot of tahini, but the bitterness works well with the chickpeas.

Remove the hummus from the blender, grate in the garlic and mix. It's good to go and be eaten as is, but I'd recommend chilling it in the fridge. I serve hummus traditionally with a little scattering of toasted cumin and smoked paprika. Toasted pine nuts are optional. But there you have it. That's your base.

EF GF VG

SERVES 4

KIRMIZI MERCİMEKLİ HUMUS Red lentil hummus

1⅔ cups (335 g) dried split red lentils
6 ice cubes
3 tbsp tahini
juice of 2½ lemons
1 garlic clove
sea salt

TO SERVE
pinch of cumin seeds, toasted and crushed
pul biber
olive oil, for drizzling

If you can't be bothered to soak chickpeas, boil them, and peel each one individually, then here's a quicker alternative.

Give the lentils a rinse in a sieve first, make sure there are no little stones. Stick the lentils in a pot big enough to cover the lentils with double the amount of water. Place over high heat and bring to a boil. Once boiling, drop the heat to medium—the water will foam, which you can skim off using a spoon. Gently cook the lentils for 20–30 minutes until soft, then drain.

Transfer the cooked lentils to a blender with a big grind of salt. It's important we season the lentils after cooking—pulses go hard if you boil them in salted water. Add the ice cubes, one by one, and blend until they have completely melted and the mixture is smooth.

The mixture will have lightened in color. Add the tahini and the juice of 2 lemons, then grate in the garlic and blend again. Check the acidity for your liking—I like a sour edge to lift the hummus. If you like the same, add the juice of the remaining lemon half. Check the seasoning and adjust with salt: no seasoning = no flavor. Spoon the hummus into a bowl. I like to finish mine with the spices on top, so sprinkle over the toasted cumin and some pul biber and drizzle with olive oil. Dip some warm bread into that son of a bitch.

EF GF VG

SERVES 4

SALATALI HUMUS Hummus with chopped salad

2 baby cucumbers
12 cherry tomatoes
½ small red onion
⅛ oz (5 g) parsley
3 sprigs of mint
½ tsp sumac
½ tsp pul biber
½ tsp cumin seeds, toasted and crushed
2 tbsp olive oil, plus extra to finish
juice of 1 lemon
sea salt

Cut the cucumbers in half and then in half again. I always take the middles out of cucumbers in case they're a little bit watery. Cube the cucumbers into little bite-sized pieces, then do the same with the tomatoes and red onion. Roughly chop through the parsley and mint.

Leave everything on the chopping board, season with a big grind of salt, plus the sumac, pul biber and toasted cumin. Add the olive oil and lemon juice and mix together by hand on the board.

Spread your hummus (see opposite) on a flat plate, make a well in the middle and stick your salad right on top. I like to drizzle over a little more olive oil, to finish.

EF GF VG

SERVES 4

After reading about what to eat in Trabzon, I was surprised to see that this was a three-ingredient salad. I went to a big köfte restaurant in the main square—to be fair, it may have been the Olive Garden equivalent of a köfte shop. I mean, it wasn't bad, just super-mainstream. I got a plate of köfte and piyaz salad: soft buttery beans, sweetness from the cherry tomatoes, crunch and texture from the lettuce and a good acidic dressing.

Straight off the bat, no canned beans here, please. Spend a little more on the beans in a glass jar that are in gloopy liquid. You can swap cannellini for navy, butter or borlotti—whatever you fancy.

PİYAZ White bean salad

- 1 cup (250 g) jarred cannellini beans, drained
- 2 heads romaine lettuce
- 12 cherry tomatoes
- ½ white onion
- olive oil, for drizzling
- ½ large lemon
- sea salt

Wash the liquid off the beans under cold water and set them aside.

Peel the romaine to get rid of the ropey outer leaves. Take the butt off the lettuce, then wash the lettuce in ice-cold water. This will keep it super-crisp and fresh. Stack the lettuce leaves on top of each other before slicing; really take your time to make sure that you're cutting them all the same size. Although this is "just a salad," there's flavor in execution and treating even the non-expensive ingredients like they broke the bank. Sharpen your knife and slice the lettuce nice and thin.

If you've got a salad spinner, GREAT! But, if like me you don't, take a clean tea towel, stick the lettuce in, then bring the edges together to make a bundle—like you're going to attach it to a stick and move out because your mom won't let you play Xbox past your bedtime. Swing the tea towel bag back and forth and the lettuce will drain. Don't do this indoors, please. Use your initiative.

Slice the cherry tomatoes in half and thinly slice the onion julienne-style, as thin as you can get them.

I build the salad on a plate. Put the lettuce down first, then the onion. Follow with the tomatoes and then the washed and drained beans.

Crack over a big bit of sea salt, zigzag over some nice peppery olive oil and squeeze with the lemon. I always mix salads with my hands. This is great with red meats, fish, or even as a little something on the side of a soup.

Kısır is often served during the warmer months of the year, fridge-cold and full of fresh crispy vegetables or in lettuce cups roadside. You can put anything in kısır—it's normally got pomegranate seeds in it, but I feel like Ottolenghi ruined pomegranate, since people started putting it in dishes willy-nilly. Big up Yotam though, he can put pomegranate on whatever he wants.

Think of this as tabbouleh's red cousin. Chop lettuce through kısır, throw in cucumbers for crunch—it's entirely up to you. This recipe makes enough to feed six, so turn up with it to a function, or take the leftovers into the office for lunch. This recipe reminds me of family get-togethers and the odd funeral—but no one has to die for you to make it.

KISIR Bulgur salad

1 mug of kısırlık (fine) bulgur
olive oil
1 lb 2 oz (500 g) white onions, finely diced
2 tbsp pul biber
1 tbsp acı toz biber (hot Turkish paprika)
1½ tbsp cumin seeds, toasted and crushed
3 tbsp tatlı biber salçası (sweet pepper paste)
2 tbsp domates salça (tomato paste)
½ tbsp sugar
½ bunch of parsley, roughly chopped
7 sprigs of mint, finely chopped
6 scallions, sliced into bite-sized pieces
3 roasted sivri biber (Turkish green peppers), finely sliced
1 large beefsteak tomato, chopped
4 tbsp pomegranate molasses
juice of 1 lemon
sea salt

Start off by cooking the bulgur. Like couscous, it's pretty much a 1:1 ratio: add a mug of bulgur to a bowl, followed by the same mug full of boiling water. Pour the water over the bulgur and add a grind of salt. Cover the bowl with a lid or plate. We want to trap the heat in as much as possible. The bulgur needs a minimum of 10 minutes to absorb the water—but I usually just leave it with a lid on until I've made the paste and finished chopping all my garnishes.

Stick a wide-based frying pan over high heat with a few splashes of olive oil; enough to coat the base of the pan. Once the oil is hot, add the onions. The heat in the pan will drop once the onions go in. Now if there's one thing that I want you to take away from these recipes, it's this: as soon as you put onions in a pan, season them with salt. The salt helps the onions to break down, release their moisture and cook more evenly. Cook the onions over medium heat for about 20 minutes. We don't want dark caramelization, we want the onions to slowly sweat and release their sweetness.

Once the onions have cooked down, add the pul biber, acı toz biber and toasted cumin. Fry the spices for 2–3 minutes until the oil in the pan starts to foam. Be careful not to burn the spices, which will make them bitter.

Next, add both your pastes and fry for another 5 minutes until the oil has soaked up all the color. The pastes will start to look grainy. Add the sugar, then check your seasoning. You want to be able to taste a balance of sweet, salty, spicy and oily. All these elements are needed to keep the eating experience exciting. Take the mixture out of the frying pan and set aside to cool.

Lay your cooked bulgur in a pan—preferably a high-sided roasting pan which makes it easier to rub everything together. Rub the paste mixture through the bulgur using your hands (a lot of these dishes are hands-on and a spoon just won't cut it—get involved and be more tactile with your food). Make sure the paste is evenly distributed and the bulgur is uniform in color.

Mix through the herbs, scallions, roasted peppers and tomato; finishing with some oil, the pomegranate molasses and lemon juice before serving.

SERVES 4

Another classic meze dish that a couple of you all-inclusive-vacation-goers probably missed. This is fried veg and a spicy sweet tomato sauce sat on top of fierce, garlicky yogurt. Yalla get the bread.

KÖPOĞLU Eggplant, peppers and garlic yogurt

9 oz (250 g) eggplants
2 Corno di Toro red peppers
4 long green Turkish peppers
4 garlic cloves, plus 1 big clove
sunflower oil, for frying
2 tbsp pul biber
1 tbsp tatlı biber salçası (sweet pepper paste)
13½ oz (380 g) tomatoes, grated
1 tbsp sugar
1⅓ cups (300 g) full-fat thick yogurt
olive oil, for drizzling
sea salt
bread, to serve

Start by peeling the eggplants in alternate sections, leaving several strips of skin ½ inch (1 cm) wide. You should be left with a pattern that resembles zebra print, or a retro 1970s pattern in your auntie's ugly house.

Slice the eggplants down the middle into 3 somewhat equal pieces, before dicing them into ¾ inch (2 cm) squares. Stick the eggplant squares in a bowl with a good amount of salt—I did 3 big pinches. Let them sit for 20 minutes to release the excess moisture. Moisture + frying = no good.

While the eggplants sit, move on to chopping the red and green peppers. Take the tops off along with the bottoms, then slice the peppers lengthways so the insides are exposed. Scrape out any seeds (they make the fryer oil dirty a lot quicker, meaning we can't use it again for other beautiful recipes in this book). Slice the peppers to a similar size as the eggplant squares; we're basically looking for bite-sized pieces, as this isn't a dish where I wanna mess around with a knife and fork. I wanna dunk bread and pull it close to my mouth as fast as possible, without dropping any on my white t-shirt.

You should have some spare time while waiting for the eggplants to let out their juices, so we can move on to making the sauce that brings everything together. Slice the 4 garlic cloves down the middle, removing any root before finely slicing as thinly and as uniformly as you can. The more uniformly we slice them, the more equally they will cook.

Over low-medium heat, coat the base of a frying pan with a glug of sunflower oil, then add the sliced garlic. We don't want instant frying; we want a soft and casual approach that will help the garlic bleed flavor, without turning to bitter garlic chips. Gently fry the garlic for 3–4 minutes, without catching any color.

Next, add the pul biber and fry for 30 seconds. Once you can smell the spice and the oil has changed color to a shiny red, go in with the pepper paste. Fry the paste off as you would with tomato paste. You want it to go from a dense paste to mingling with the garlic—spreading and allowing its flavor to be soaked up by the punchy garlicky oil we've made.

CONTINUES OVERLEAF

When I say use grated tomato, I mean you need to have sliced a tomato down the middle and worked the flesh side against the biggest side of a box grater. You'll be left with pulp in a bowl and the tomato skin in your hand. Add the tomato pulp to the pan, which at this point will be hot. The noise of the tomato hitting the heat will be loud and aggressive, but it's cool because pretty much straight after that, the temperature will drop and the tomatoes will slowly start to blip away. Give it a good stir to combine the spicy paste and the tomatoes.

We want to cook off all that water the tomatoes have expressed. Once the tomato water is cooked off and the sauce starts to thicken, add a big grind of salt along with the sugar. Leave the tomato sauce to simmer over a low heat, stirring occasionally to ensure it doesn't catch—we want to keep it warm so there is a contrast of hot and cold elements in this dish.

Using a pot with high sides or a deep cast-iron pan, add enough oil to deep-fry our vegetables. They aren't huge so we won't need loads—filling a third of the way up will do. Remember that the oil will become thinner, looser and less dense once up to temperature. Heat the oil to about 350°F (180°C).
For best results, check the temperature using a thermometer.

Drain and discard any collected moisture from the eggplants and place the first batch in to fry. I said batch—please do not be a cowboy and put them all in at once. If you do that, then the temperature in the pan will drop and the eggplants will remain little pale, oily bits. That's not good enough—we've just taken great care to let them sit for 20 minutes, for fuck's sake. Look after them. Fry off the eggplants until crispy, brown and soft.

Remove the eggplants from the oil and lay the pieces to rest on a plate lined with paper towels, to absorb the excess grease. Remember to season while they're still warm. Once all the pieces of eggplant have been fried, you can repeat the process with the peppers. The peppers also have a high water content, so be careful as you put them into the oil, to avoid splash-back.
Fry the peppers until the skins are starting to peel and the flesh is soft.
Again, allow them to rest on some paper towels before seasoning with salt.

Last prep stage: grate the big garlic clove into the yogurt and mix it in.

To build, I like to use a plate with a lip; it's up to you whether you make one massive platter or a couple of smaller dishes to spread across the table for guests. Either way, smooth your yogurt to coat the base.

Pile the eggplants and peppers on top of the yogurt, giving the dish some height. Spoon over the hot, sweet tomato sauce. I like to follow this with a little zigzag of good olive oil for the bitterness. Dunk your bread in that and enjoy.

EF GF VG

SERVES 2

I love a humble roasted shallot recipe and this one is so simple; it's great eaten hot in the winter or cold in the summer. In the UK, we're lucky to get different varieties of shallot all year round, including banana shallots and round ones. If, however, you can't get hold of any, a good old-fashioned white onion works just as well.

KAVRULMUŞ SOĞAN Roasted shallots

1 lb 2 oz (500 g) round shallots, unpeeled
1 heaped tsp sumac
1 tsp acı toz biber (hot Turkish paprika)
3 tbsp olive oil
2 tbsp pomegranate molasses
sea salt
a few sprigs of flat-leaf parsley, to garnish

Preheat the oven to 425°F (220°C).

Stick the shallots on a baking sheet, just as they are, no need to season or oil. Bake for 45 minutes–1 hour until they are nice and soft.

Pull the shallots out of the oven and leave them to rest until they are cool enough to be handled.

Next, we're going to peel the shallots. The easiest way to do this is by removing the bottom end of the root with a sharp knife, to expose the layers. Peel back the outer skin plus the first layer underneath, which is normally quite tough. The rest of the shallot can be squeezed out from the top, which keeps the layers unbroken in their petal shape.

Once all the shallots are peeled into separate layers, place them in a bowl. Add a big crack of sea salt, along with the sumac and acı toz biber. Go in with the oil and the pomegranate molasses before gently mixing together.

Transfer to a serving dish and add a few sprigs of parsley as a nice color break to garnish. Serve either alone as a starter or with grilled meat and bread.

Turks love a pickle, normally a lacto-ferment which is basically salt and water, but we don't have six months, so we're going with vinegar here. I pretty much always use the 3-2-1 method: three parts vinegar, two parts sugar, one part water. It's the easiest way to pickle.

LAHANA TURŞUSU Pickled red cabbage

- 1 large red cabbage, trimmed
- 2 tbsp sea salt
- 2⅓ cups (560 ml) grape or red wine vinegar
- scant 1½ cups (280 g) sugar
- 1½ tbsp fine sea salt
- 1 tsp fennel seeds
- 1 tsp coriander seeds
- ½ tsp black peppercorns
- 2 tsp pul biber
- scant 1 cup (195 ml) water

Start off by shredding the cabbage. I do this on a mandoline and I go just a bit thicker than you would for a coleslaw so the pickle is ready to eat within a couple of hours. By all means go thick-cut on the cabbage, but be aware it will need a longer salting time and a longer pickling time, so it's up to you, babes.

Once the cabbage is shredded and in a bowl, add the salt to draw out the moisture and crisp up the cabbage. Let it sit for at least 1 hour.

Meanwhile, let's make the pickle. Add the vinegar, sugar, salt and spices to a saucepan. Bring the pickling liquid to a boil, then pour the hot pickle into the water through a sieve, straining any spices out. We just want the flavor, no one wants to bite into a whole fucking peppercorn. Let the pickling liquid sit until the cabbage is ready.

When the hour is up, squeeze the cabbage in your hands, wearing gloves if you don't wanna stain your hands or you just got a manicure. Squeeze the cabbage as much as you can to get out as much water as possible. Discard the water.

Pour the pickling liquid over the red cabbage and seal in sterilized containers or clean Tupperware. Pickles will keep for up to 3 months, unopened, if refrigerated and stored in a sterilized container. Consume within two weeks of opening.

EF GF VG

SERVES 4

There's a good ezme recipe in my first book, but I came across this one on my travels that had a popular Turkish drink in it called vişne, or sour cherry juice to you and me. It's a drink I grew up on. I ate this in a little kebap shop called Hacı Hanifoğulları Pirzola ve Kebap Salonu, where I sat in a tiny room above the mangal, with smoke creeping up the stairs. Everything looked like something my dad would have built—crooked walls, repurposed furniture, outside tables indoors. Anyway, this recipe makes a great little BBQ side; the longer it sits, the better it gets.

EZME Turkish salsa

- 3 kapya or red peppers (one for grilling, the rest kept raw)
- 1 red chile
- 1 green chile
- 2 cucumbers
- 3 green Charleston hot peppers
- 2 scallions
- generous 1 cup (250 ml) vişne (sour cherry juice)
- 4 tbsp olive oil
- 2 tbsp pomegranate molasses
- juice of ½ lemon
- sea salt

I find that fire-roasting one of the kapya peppers and the chiles gives you a sweeter flavor and a good hum of heat. If you don't have the BBQ lit, you can do this over a gas flame—just make sure you turn them often enough so they don't completely burn. Alternatively, throw them in an oven at 475°F (240°C) and give them a roast for 15 minutes until the flesh is soft and the skin is blistered. If you do have the BBQ lit, don't cook the living shit out of them. Blister the skins and you'll see the peppers and chiles start to expand. Transfer them to a bowl, cover in plastic wrap and leave to steam.

Once cool, peel and deseed before finely dicing. When I say finely dice, I mean really small, like anally small. Leave no chunky bits—we want everything to be uniform in size.

Peel the cucumbers lengthways in alternate sections, leaving several strips of skin ½ inch (1 cm) wide. You should be left with a pattern that resembles zebra print. Remove the seeds, then deseed the raw peppers, too. Cut the cucumbers, peppers and scallions as small as you've cut the roasted peppers. Please don't do this in a blender for fuck's sake. Blenders are great for some things but we want to take care of our ezme. Make sure you're not bruising the hell out of the veg. I don't cut corners with food, those lazy chefs I've worked with never got book deals for a reason. It's all about respecting the product.

Stick all your raw and cooked veg into a bowl. Season first with salt, then add the vişne, olive oil, pomegranate molasses and lemon juice. The liquid will look a bit much at the start, but the longer it sits, the more the veg sucks up the moisture and starts to break down. Honestly delicious—sweet, sour, fiery and crunchy.

EF GF VG

SERVES 4

This is one of those dishes where you begin to understand the beauty and simplicity of food; the kind of recipe I enjoy the most. Humble ingredients, slap bang in their prime—all you've gotta do is cook them right. This dish is usually served with rakı in little fish restaurants in Istanbul. When you go to a meyhane in Türkiye and before you've even had a chance to look at the menu, bread is delivered to the table, plates are turned over and two waiters come rushing to the table—one with a pen and paper in hand and the other tilting a tray of meze wrapped in plastic wrap. They'll point to each one, explaining what it is and you just say yes or no. You get to see the choice and know what you're in for.

I enjoy the fact that Turks, like the Italians, celebrate vegetables when in season. In Türkiye's early spring, when the artichokes are out, men stand shouting at stalls, peeling artichokes for this dish and, the more commonly eaten, dolma. I've spent years in restaurants peeling artichokes until my hands were black and everything tasted bitter for the rest of the day. You've not gotta peel many for this recipe, but saying that, I still think you should glove up.

I used multicolored carrots here, they were organic and I got them from a bougie farmers' market. If you can't find fresh fava beans, I'd recommend swapping them for peas. With this recipe being all about celebrating spring, get them fresh.

ENGİNAR Artichokes

5 globe artichokes
2½ lemons
6 skinny carrots
1¾ oz (50 g) fresh fava beans, unpodded
olive oil, for drizzling
sea salt and pepper

The easiest way to explain how to peel an artichoke is the "she loves me, she loves me not" method. You know in school, when you'd pick the petals off a flower, daydreaming about whether she was into you. Not me, boy—I was tough as nails, but you know what I mean. From the base of the artichoke, pick the leaves individually, pulling them downwards until they naturally snap. Keep doing this until the leaves start to get lighter and you can see the heart of the artichoke forming. This normally looks like an arrow; pointy at the top but with a thick base. Cut the pointy part off the artichoke where it stops. If you've peeled enough, you will clearly see what I mean; if not, keep peeling, you're not there yet. Once there, the inside of the artichoke will be full of choke. Using a teaspoon, scoop out all the choke. Once the choke is out, use very little pressure on the spoon to scrape away that first layer of flesh where the choke was connected. There's loads of little hair follicles there. Just scrape them away. Trim the stalk of the artichoke so it's about 1 inch (2.5 cm) long.

CONTINUES OVERLEAF

When you start messing around with artichokes, the flesh reacts with the air, slowly turning them black or brown. As soon as you've prepped an artichoke, it needs to go in a big bowl of water with 2 of the lemons squeezed into it to stop them from discoloring.

Peel the carrots, trying to keep them circular. Split all the carrots down the middle and set to one side. Pop the fava beans out of their pods and set them to one side, too.

Now there's not much to the cooking here. Stick the artichokes in a pot with fresh water. Add salt to the water and taste it—it should be salty. The last thing we want is to spend all that time asking yourself if she loves you and then not seasoning the spiky little bastards.

Bring the artichokes to a boil, then simmer for about 8 minutes until you can get a knife into the stalk with a little resistance. Once cooked, stick them in a bowl of ice-cold water to cool.

Get rid of the artichoke water and fill the pot again with enough salt for it to be salty. Bring the water to a boil and add your carrots. Boil the carrots depending on their size—I had little skinny ones so mine were done in about 4 minutes, but like the artichokes, we still want texture to our carrots, so don't boil them to fuck. When the carrots are about a minute away from being cooked, add the fava beans. Stick the carrots and fava beans in the same ice-cold water as the artichokes, just make sure it's still ice-cold and the heat from the artichokes hasn't warmed it. The vegetables don't need to be in there long. We're stopping the cooking process, so they just need to be cold.

Drain and dry all the veg on a couple of clean kitchen cloths. Pop the fava beans out of their skins so they're vibrant and green, some will come out as a whole bean and some will have split. Not a problem, don't worry about it. Cut the artichokes into quarters.

I stacked the vegetables on a plate, then seasoned them with a good sprinkle of salt and a couple of grinds of black pepper. Zigzag over some nice punchy olive oil and serve with the remaining ½ lemon (cut into wedges) for squeezing over the top. It might sound boring, but honestly, eat this on one of those long spring evenings and it doesn't really need anything else.

EF GF V

SERVES 4

I ate this waiting for a kebap in a pretty restaurant in a fancy part of Istanbul overlooking a main road. I was seriously underdressed, but I've never dressed up to eat a kebap in my life. It was in a part of Istanbul that was the equivalent of Knightsbridge, London: fake lips, butt lifts, ugly designer shoes and expensive clutch bags. Full of people that eat in expensive places for the "vibe" and not for the food. Most of the time when I make these peppers, I'm in the at-home Turkish uncle uniform: white tank, shorts, socks and sandals, dirty-ish tea towel over the shoulder and a BBQ squint from the heat of the mangal.

ATOM Yogurt-dressed peppers

6 red long peppers, such as Corno di Toro or kapya
6 red chiles
1 garlic clove
1 lb (450 g) strained yogurt
sea salt

TO SERVE (OPTIONAL)
pul biber
olive oil
pomegranate molasses

I always cook peppers and chiles over fire for that deep smoky flavor, and you're going to want to, too. If not, over a gas flame at home is fine or roast them in a hot oven on the highest heat. Whichever way you decide to do it (oven being the safest), make sure the peppers and chiles are cooked all the way through, and are blistered and floppy. I don't bother with seasoning them or rubbing them with oil.

Peel the skins off the peppers and chiles. Now, I'm really anal when it comes to seeds, so make sure you've taken all the seeds out of both. Give them a rough chop—you want bite-sized pieces. Pat them dry on paper towels or with a clean kitchen cloth.

Stick them in a bowl with a couple of big grinds of salt, grate in the garlic and add the yogurt. Give it a good mix and taste—you want it to be sweet, with a background of garlic, cool from the yogurt and finished with a little heat but nothing major. This can sit in the fridge for a good 3 days, so making it in advance isn't a problem.

To serve, I pile the mixture on to a plate, add a lot of pul biber since I like it hot—when something is advertised with the word chile, I wanna feel it—a swirl of olive oil and a little bit of pomegranate molasses. This is great on its own but I like the little bit of sweetness you get from the molasses.

It's great spread on toast, as a good table dip or something to take to a BBQ.

YENGE'NIN PANCARI Auntie Yenge's beets

We're used to getting beets in vacuum bags with a light dressing or shredded in little plastic pots as "salad boosters." But it's time to pay beets some respect, man, it's not a bottom-of-the-league vegetable. When you buy them in season, they're fresh, earthy, sweet and a beautiful color.

There's a decent drinking culture in Istanbul, though I wouldn't say it's the same all over Türkiye. In Istanbul, you can walk into a convenience store and get whatever you like. There are plenty of bars, clubs and pubs. Empty blue beer crates sit outside shops. In Türkiye, the bottles go back to the factory, where they're washed and refilled. With parts of Türkiye where the religious outweigh the non-religious, it's a little more difficult to get alcohol freely. You have to go to an alcohol-specific shop, and I didn't see that many. While drinking stupid amounts of rakı one night in Istanbul alone during a mid-life-crisis-wife-left-me thing, I was served a plate of oddly-cut chunky beets, dressed in olive oil and vinegar, and I really enjoyed it, taking notes on my phone, thinking about what I could do with it.

On the last leg of my travels, I decided to fly over to Cyprus from Adana to write an intro and check in on my family. I had lunch with my Auntie Yenge and Uncle Hasan, whom I'm named after. The word *yenge* in Turkish means an auntie who has married into the family. My auntie was going on about how she had grown these beets and insisted I try them. Cyprus is like that:

"Let me get you a plate of food."
"No thank you Auntie, I've just eaten."
"I've made the jam, you should try it."
"No thank you Auntie, I've eaten."
"Hasan, you've come all this way, I can't let you starve."
"No Auntie, I've eaten."

The food questioning continuing like two boxers exchanging jabs and, before you know it, she's hit you with a big left hand and you're sitting at the table, paper towels tucked into your t-shirt, with a bowl of beet salad in front of you, with half a loaf of bread. Sucker punch.

My Auntie Yenge served hers up with a spiky vinegar dressing, loads of freshly cracked black pepper and a handful of fresh cilantro from her humble little garden. The leaves on the beets I bought weren't any good, but if you've got leaves and they're stiff and fresh-looking, add them to the recipe—treat them like you would chard—a quick blanch in heavily salted water. Great stuff.

CONTINUES OVERLEAF

2 lb (900 g) beets
⅔ cup (150 ml) grape or red wine vinegar

FOR THE DRESSING

pinch of sugar
½ cup (120 ml) grape or red wine vinegar
10 cherry tomatoes
4 scallions
¼ oz (10 g) cilantro leaves
7 tbsp good-quality olive oil
feta or beyaz peynir (optional)
salt and pepper

Give the beets a good scrub to make sure you've got rid of any dirt. Stick the beets in the biggest pot you've got, cover them in about 2 inches (5 cm) of water and season the water heavily with salt, as if you were gonna cook pasta.

Bring the beets to a boil and add the ⅔ cup (150 ml) of vinegar. I like to get that vinegar flavor into the beets while cooking. Beets are big, chunky vegetables, so adding a little vinegar in now will mean that they'll take on the dressing better. Gently simmer the beets for about 30 minutes. We want to cook them just until you can put a fork through them with very little resistance. The simmering time will vary on the size of your beets; when buying them in bunches, try to get ones that are somewhat of an even size.

Drain the beets and just leave them in a colander to cool; they'll continue to cook while they rest. When the beets are cool enough to handle, peel the skins away under cold running water. You should be able to do this with your thumb. The skins are tough and it will look like you're peeling away loads, but don't worry, you're not. I like to neaten the beets up a little by trimming where the leaves were attached and taking off the stringy roots.

Cut the beets into bite-sized pieces; I did some in quarters and others in halves before putting them in a bowl. Season with a generous handful of salt and pepper, plus the pinch of sugar. Add the vinegar next and give them a good stir.

Chop in the cherry tomatoes and scallions; in true Cyprus-style, I cut them in my hand over the bowl. Go in with the cilantro next, giving it a rough chop, and finish with the olive oil. Just a side note, if you've got a bit of feta or beyaz peynir knocking about, cube that up and stick it in, too. Very good stuff.

250 00

03

FISH

KUMKAPI (Istanbul, Northern Türkiye)

Kumkapı is the center of the Armenian community of Istanbul. The one thing you've gotta eat here is turbot. Turks call it *kalkan* in their language. Me and Hus once had an argument on vacation in Istanbul, at the restaurant Neyzen which is slap bang in the middle of the strip, about how our turbot should be cooked. Obviously, I wanted it grilled but Hus wanted it fried—so we asked politely if we could do half and half, and they gave us what we wanted. Out came the turbot, on a bed of lettuce with some quartered onions and a couple of lemon wedges. Hus knew immediately I'd been right, and I knew he knew that—but we enjoyed the fish in peace. Grilled always is better—although there is always a place in my stomach for lightly-fried meaty fish in cornmeal on the right occasion.

Going back to Neyzen on my own is weird. This time, I'm sitting by my lonesome with a medium-sized bottle of rakı. Four mezes down, on the cusp of being drunk, I decide to order the smallest turbot they had in the window. It's not a whopper, but a respectable 3 lb (1.3 kg). I ask for it grilled, and the waiter asks me if I'm sure. Of course I'm sure, man! This fish would cost me at least £150 ($200) at Brat back in London. Just let me eat my turbot grilled, please. I plough through, eating little bits of onion to break up the richness of the fatty fish, with a little drunk smile and a big hunk of bread. I have to be honest: I can't eat it all, but luckily there's an abundance of stray cats in Kumkapı. I feed them the head, a couple of fillets and most of the collar. Hands covered in sticky turbot fat, a whole bottle of rakı down, and a stomach full of mostly bread—it's time for me to go home.

I spend a lot of time over my three weeks in Istanbul feeding strays—mostly the dogs, because I miss my boy, Denzil. Every night, on the bus from Eminonu back to Beyoglu, I check on three dogs I befriended; feeding them bits of leftovers wrapped in tissue paper from restaurants or takeout places. I don't really feel homesick while I'm here, but if I do, I go out looking for the dogs, feed the stray cats or mop the floor in my apartment. I grew up in a house that always smelled like fabric softener and was (nearly) always spotless. So when I have days when I can't face walking or eating any more Turkish food, I stick all my laundry in the machine with loads of fabric softener, before mopping the floors to make it feel like Mom had been here.

I like to people-watch at airports and look out for sunburned tourists, wondering whether or not they ate good food on their trip. On leaving Istanbul, about to jump on a short flight to Trabzon full of Turks, I'm beginning to accept the fact that I'm always gonna stand out like a sore thumb here. Is it my tall, godly physique? Is it my feminine, curled eyelashes? Or is it just the fact I look like a big, German tourist with leg tattoos and a fanny pack? Fanny packs (I like to call them "man bags" to make me sound less like an American) should strictly only be used for two things: vacations, or day festivals in Hackney Wick where you chew the inside of your mouth and everyone's ears off to heavy baselines and MDMA. I'm a shorts and a hoodie man—it's not a show-off-tattoos thing. I'd call my dress sense "hood comfort." Luckily, I've packed full-length pants to at least try and blend in as I journey on—legs out is the international sign of a tourist and, although I wear shorts all year round, these guys didn't know that.

5A

EF GF

SERVES 4

Turks have a thing for stuffing things—their face, vegetables and meat into bread. It only makes sense that someone saw a mussel and was like,"bet that would be better stuffed." Stuffed mussels are everywhere you look in Istanbul, usually being sold by a young teen trying to make a quick buck down the side roads off Taksim Square, at Eminönü with floating fish guys, or at the fish market in Kadıköy. Istanbul has the feeling that everyone is on an episode of *The Apprentice*, trying to make a quick flip on a business idea. You don't need a permit to rock up somewhere and sell food; you just need customers and a good-quality product. The price, size, taste and quality varies from vendor to vendor. If you are off to Istanbul anytime soon, this is a dish to seek out for sure. You've gotta try it by the Bosphorus, sitting on a bench with salt in the air, while someone's playing the violin, men are fishing and flags are swinging in the wind. I'm not gonna lie, it's kinda magical.

OK, enough sentimental shit. I used sushi rice for this; baldo rice is a bit temperamental and the starch in sushi rice helps when it comes to the stuffing.

MIDYE DOLMA Stuffed mussels

- 4 lb 8 oz (2 kg) mussels in shell
- 1 mug of sushi rice
- 2 small white onions
- olive oil, for frying
- 3 tsp freshly cracked black pepper
- 1 heaped tsp ground allspice
- sea salt
- 2 lemons, to serve

Part 1: mussel prep. Pull off any stringy bits from the middle of the mussels. Scrape anything on the outside of the mussels with a butter knife. Now it's important that we clean the mussels properly—this isn't a rinse with a dribble of water like you're eating an apple. If any of those mussels have dirt in them or around them, all of this work will be for nothing. I can't tell you how much I hate eating a mussel, scallop or a clam and finding a bit of sand. It really puts me off.

Now that your mussels are clean, using a knife with a pointed tip (it doesn't have to be sharp), poke your way into the mussel on the side that the beard was on. Once your knife is in, run it all the way round the mussel until you can pop it open. They won't open completely, so you have to give them a little gentle crack so they can lay flat. Do this over a bowl so that any juice that comes out of the mussel can be used to steam them open. Free flavor. Once all the mussels are open, there's a little bit in the middle of the meat that looks like a pit or a seed—cut or pull this off. Rinse all the mussels again, getting rid of any murky water left behind; do this thoroughly, too. No grit please, I beg you. Stick the mussels in the fridge and get on with the rice.

CONTINUES OVERLEAF

Measure a mug of rice, any mug, doesn't matter. Wash that rice until the water runs clear. Gently move the rice around with a claw-shaped hand. A good 5 minutes of washing is plenty. Once the rice is washed, put it in a bowl, cover with loads of fresh water and let it soak for 30 minutes.

Finely dice the onions. Now as this is going into our rice, when I say finely diced, I mean like the onions in a Big Mac, or when you watch a Michelin-starred chef cut a shallot, that's how small I'm talking. We want the sweetness from the onion but no bite. Sweat the onions in a heavy-based pot in a decent amount of olive oil (I don't believe in measuring, it's fucking boring), over medium heat with 2 big grinds of salt. Sweat the onions with no color for about 30 minutes until soft and translucent. You gotta be patient here man, if you do this over high heat your onions will release sugars too early and get crispy brown and bitter. Look after the onions and they'll look after you. Promise.

Once the onions are soft and sweet, drain the rice and stick it in the pot. Fry off the rice over medium heat—we really just want to cook off any excess moisture. Add the black pepper and allspice and fry that for a minute or so. Now, using the same mug you used for the rice, add a mug of cold water. Add a little splash of olive oil and a big grind of salt. Cover and bring to a boil. Once boiling, transfer to the smallest burner on your stovetop (or if you're using induction, the lowest setting) and steam the rice over very low heat for 8 minutes.

The rice will be undercooked at 8 minutes but it's cool, trust me. Once the timer is done, kill the heat and let your rice steam for 5 minutes. Please don't lift the lid to see if it's working. Just trust me. I've got you. After 5 minutes, lay your rice out flat on a tray or something similar to help it cool. We need the rice to be cool before it goes into the shells.

Once the rice has cooled, take 1 teaspoon of your mixture, or enough to fill one side of the shell of your mussel. Then push the mussels back together again until they close. If they don't close you've either not got enough rice in them or you haven't broken the shells in half completely. Once the mussels are stuffed and closed, lay them somewhat neatly into a pot. I used the same pot I cooked the rice in. Stick the pot over a high heat, add in any reserved mussel juice and 4 tablespoons of water. Cover the mussels and steam over high heat for 5 minutes. Turn off the heat and let them sit.

You've gotta serve these with loads of lemons—cut the lemons however you want, just make sure there are enough to squeeze a little juice on every mussel. You'll be surprised how many of these you can actually eat. I ate thirty once with the boys in Türkiye. Good times.

SERVES 1

As soon as you get to Istanbul, you have to eat balık ekmek on the seafront at Eminönü. It's a mackerel sandwich and one of the first things I properly fell in love with there. The vibe in Eminönü can be very in your face: there are people selling simit (Turkish bagels), commuters catching boats to work and young boys pressuring you to buy pickle juice. There's a smell of coal-roasted chestnuts in the air, mixed with the saltiness of the Bosphorus. Although we have this romantic idea that fish is caught just hours before you eat it, it's often not the truth. The mackerel I ate in Eminönü was most probably frozen on board a Norwegian ship, to keep the cost of an affordable lunch down. The meaning of the word "affordable" changes according to where you are in the world. A mackerel sandwich in Eminönü will set you back 240tl, which is about $6.

I can't stress the importance of buying quality ingredients for fish recipes. Get yourself a line-caught mackerel, still shiny with a blueish pattern, similar to leopard print. A lot of people don't really mess with mackerel. I've often heard "It's too fishy" or "It's too oily." Only old mackerel is fishy, and it can't be helped that it's an oily fish. Mackerel is normally cooked on a plancha but, you know me—get the BBQ lit, son. The oiliness works well with the BBQ smoke. We want to trap all that flavor into our soft, crispy, warm bread.

BALIK EKMEK Mackerel sandwich

- 1 mackerel, filleted and pin-boned
- olive oil, for drizzling
- ½ loaf of Turkish sandwich bread (or baguette), cut down the middle
- 3 romaine lettuce leaves, finely sliced
- ¼ white onion, finely sliced
- ½ lemon
- sea salt

TO SERVE (OPTIONAL)

- lacto-fermented pickles
- pickled chiles (see page 29 for homemade)

Make yourself a little prep station on a tray, so all the ingredients are laid out in front of you, ready to use. There isn't loads of prep for this sandwich to come together, but that doesn't mean you should turn your nose up and think you're better than it. Cooking fish right isn't always easy and the reason these are so good in Eminönü is because it goes: warm fish into bread, then add the garnish. There's no fuck-around time washing lettuce or trying to finely slice an onion slowly. Get that shit done first. So rinse your mackerel and pat it with paper towels until completely dry. Put a couple of pinches of salt into a ramekin dish. Line up your bottle of olive oil and the bread. Wear your socks and slides and, if you can be bothered, stick on some Turkish folk music. Set the vibe.

With mackerel being an oily fish already, you won't need to add loads of olive oil. Add a very little splash of oil to the skin side and rub it in with your fingers. If you don't do this, I promise you the mackerel will stick to the grill and your trip to the fishmonger will no longer be worth it.

When the BBQ is at a 2 count (see "How to Light a BBQ," page 246), season the mackerel skin with salt and lay the fillets, skin-side down, on the grill. Wherever they land, that's where they're staying. If you try and move them now, then the flesh will stick and tear.

Let the fish cook for 3 minutes on the skin side. You'll see the change in color start at the very edge of the mackerel first, then the rest of the flesh will begin to turn from light brown to bright white. Stick your bread on top of the grill to warm it through and catch the smoke.

When the color has changed halfway up the fish, it's time to flip so that the fillets face down. The mackerel only really needs 35–45 seconds to cook on the fillet side, until the meat is white and firm. Pull the mackerel off the grill and let it rest inside the bread, to soak up all the juices.

Add the lettuce and onion to your sandwich. Top with a little grind of salt and a squeeze of lemon juice. Close the sandwich and compress between your hands with a gentle squash, so the bread absorbs all that flavor.

The sandwich doesn't need much else before serving, but a couple of lacto-fermented pickles and a couple of pickled chiles wouldn't go amiss.

Until I went to Istanbul to research this book, I hadn't visited in about five years. Not much had changed, still the same smells, still the hustle and bustle of a largely populated city with hungry stomachs, still men selling simit on street corners, still people fishing in the Bosphorus. But, what I did notice, was that there wasn't just balık ekmek (see page 80) being sold in Eminönü any more. Balık ekmek (mackerel sandwich) had evolved into balık dürüm (mackerel wrap).

A new contender in the block, it's safe to say balık dürüm was great. There were a few differences between this new variation and old-school balık ekmek: the large soft, crusty rolls had been replaced with thin, elastic lavaş flatbread, plus mountains of spice rub that no one would disclose the ingredients of. Once the durum was rolled, it was sprayed with a light showering of soy sauce, using a water bottle with a pierced cap.

BALIK DÜRÜM New-school mackerel wrap

- 1 mackerel, filleted and pin-boned
- olive oil, for drizzling
- 1 lavaş
- 3 romaine lettuce leaves, whole
- ¼ white onion, finely sliced
- juice of ½ lemon
- 2 tablespoons soy sauce
- sea salt

FOR THE RUB

- 1 tsp sesame seeds, toasted
- ¼ tsp sweet paprika
- ¼ tsp nigella seeds
- ½ tsp cumin seeds, toasted
- ¼ tsp coriander seeds
- ½ tsp dried flowering oregano
- 1 tsp dried mint
- 1 tsp pul biber

Pat-dry your mackerel with a clean, dry tea towel before splashing the skin with a little olive oil and salt. Get a prep tray ready and use it to combine all the ingredients for the mackerel rub.

Grill the mackerel over a 3 count (see page 246), using the same method we did for the balık ekmek (see pages 80–81)

Once the mackerel has been flipped, start warming the lavaş on the grill for about 1 minute.

Once the mackerel is cooked and the lavaş is warm, place the mackerel in the middle of the lavaş and top with the lettuce, onion and lemon juice.

Roll up the lavaş just like a fajita, ensuring you've tucked in the ends to prevent any leakage. Using a pastry brush, coat the wrap with a generous layer of the soy sauce.

Place the lavaş back on the grill and let the wrap cook for about a minute until it catches some color and the bread is crispy. Flip the wrap a couple of times throughout cooking to ensure it gets an even color.

Pull the wrap off the grill and go in with a second brushing of the remaining soy sauce, just on one side of the bread.

While the soy sauce is still wet, sprinkle the dry rub down the center, like an airport's landing strip. That's it: new-school mackerel wrap.

SERVES 4

CALAMARI

Fried squid reminds me of summer nights in Cyprus. On the very few times we would go out for dinner as a family, we would often have fish, and there would always be a huge plate of calamari with a couple of wedges of lemon being handed around. If I'm in a restaurant, nine times out of ten I'll order the fish. There's such beauty in eating a piece of really fresh fish, cooked just to the point where it's holding together.

Calamari comes in loads of different forms, but when testing this recipe I tried it with just polenta. I tried making batters, seasoning flours, marinating the calamari in milk and loads of different things that I've picked up in restaurants. But I settled with the method that was most nostalgic for me. I said to Mom after frying the first ring and trying it, "Doesn't that taste like Cyprus?," and she agreed. Now I know this book is about Türkiye, but a lot of the calamari I ate in Türkiye brought back the same memories for me. I don't think there's anything unique about calamari in Cyprus. It's more the fact that it's been caught in the sea you're looking at while eating it. Anyway, island vibes are doing something with squid, and it's almost always deep-fried. Some were crisp, some soggy but all were equally delicious. I don't like to complicate dishes, nor am I the type to fuck with simple ingredients. This calamari is dedicated to that one semi-drunk night I had in Kumkapı.

Get your fishmonger to do the hard work. Ask for your calamari cleaned and cut into calamari rings. To be honest, I don't believe in frozen fish, only shrimp, so please do this with a fresh bit of squid. Yes, I know squid can be expensive, but this isn't something that you're gonna make for a dinner party or for five people. Cook this just for the household. Also, calamari isn't just an appetizer. Serve it with store-bought sides, such as hummus, cacık, other dips, a well-dressed salad and crispy bread. If you can afford to make this as an app, well done, you've succeeded in life, but for the rest of us, this is tonight's dinner.

I like my squid simple, with a grind of salt and a wedge of lemon, but in Türkiye it's often served with a sweet yogurt dip, sometimes with walnuts or dill. I'm gonna give you the very basic way of doing it. Feel free to add capers and cornichons and make it a kind of tartare, or try it with walnuts.

CONTINUES OVERLEAF

1 lb 7 oz (650 g) cleaned squid tentacles, separated and cut into finger-width rings
½ tbsp sugar
1 tsp baking soda
scant 1½ cups (330 ml) sparkling water
scant 1 cup (200 ml) sunflower or vegetable oil
juice of 1 lemon, to serve
sea salt

FOR THE BATTER
1⅔ cups (200 g) all-purpose flour, plus extra for dusting
¾ cup (120 g) fine polenta
1⅔ cups (400 ml) sparkling water, chilled

FOR THE DIP (OPTIONAL)
⅔ cup (160 g) full-fat thick yogurt
½ tsp sugar
juice of 1 lemon

When you get back from the fishmongers, wash the prepped calamari in a sieve with cold water, making sure there's no gloopy squid left inside the rings. Now, after talking to different chefs in Türkiye and doing a little research, Turks wash their calamari in sparkling water with a little bit of baking soda and let it sit. So, add the sugar and baking soda to a bowl, then add the squid and the sparkling water. The baking soda and the sparkling water will react and foam for a couple seconds. Give the squid a good swim in this mixture and let it sit until you're ready to cook; if you're cooking straight away, 10 minutes is plenty.

This batter is basically a tempura with polenta in it to give it the yellow color and flavor you get on those all-inclusive vacations to Marmaris or Bodrum. It's super-important that the sparkling water is proper cold, so stick it in the freezer for a bit. The reason for this is that the cold batter hits the hot oil and immediately starts to puff and cook, which adds to the crispness.

In a high-sided pot, heat enough oil to cook the calamari to 340–350°F (170–180°C). You want enough oil for the squid to be just submerged so the squid can fry completely. The batter will make the squid float to the top, so we need enough oil to make sure the squid doesn't stick to the bottom of the pot—about 2 inches (5 cm) is plenty.

In a bowl, mix the all-purpose flour with the polenta. Pour in the bubbly water, little by little; the first bit of water will make the flour mixture clumpy, but it will loosen by the time all the liquid is in. Once the tempura is made, you wanna use it straight away. To keep it cold, sit the bowl in another bowl with ice and water.

Drain, then dry the squid that's been in the baking soda liquid with a clean kitchen cloth or some paper towels. Season the squid with salt; I find this easier than just putting salt into flour willy nilly.

Lightly coat the squid rings and tentacles in flour and shake them to get rid of any excess flour. Dip the squid into the batter and hold it above the bowl to let it drip off any excess. Gently dip half the squid into the hot oil away from you and watch it fry for about 10 seconds, then gently drop the squid in. Don't just drop it in from a high height or you'll get splash-back. Just remember, you're in control.

If you've done this correctly, when you add the squid to the hot oil, the squid should float to the top. Repeat this with all the squid, cooking in batches. The squid needs room to fry and let the batter go crispy.

Fry the squid for about 4 minutes a side until golden brown and crispy. Done.

If you want to serve with the dip, just mix all the ingredients together and season with a good grind of salt and some lemon juice, if you like.

SERVES 3

I'd never even heard of fish köfte until I went to a viral fish restaurant in Trabzon and was pleasantly surprised. The köfte in Türkiye was just minced fish bits, and from a restaurant perspective that makes sense to use all the trimmings that are going in the trash to make money. Now, none of us have fish trimmings kicking around at home unless one of your parents is a fisherman, fisherwoman or a fisherthey/them. So, I went with that good old English classic haddock, and cod's meatier cousin, salmon, which is probably the most bought fish in supermarkets, plus frozen shrimp, which I always have in my freezer for a quick noodle dinner. I'll leave my *Quick Dinners with Has* book until I've fully sold out and get a team to do it for me. But for now, this is it. Just a boy, sitting alone in a fish restaurant, trying to figure out how he's going to make this shit accessible.

Now you'll see in the ingredients list that I've put tail fat in my köfte and that's because I didn't want to add eggs or breadcrumbs to bring the mixture together. Too many breadcrumbs and you don't get delicious fish juices, and eggs take on a weird color and don't really work well on a BBQ. So, I thought like a Turk and added some fat to help bind the mixture together. Not only does it help hold the köfte together but as that fat renders we're gonna get a delicious smoke. Any lamb fat will do but just make sure it's cold. It doesn't add anything to the flavor, but it makes sure our köftes don't dry out and we get a really good smoke going.

BALIK KÖFTESI Fish köfte

- 14 oz (400 g) haddock, skinned
- 12 oz (350 g) salmon, skinned
- 10 frozen shrimp, defrosted, peeled and deveined
- ½ oz (15 g) parsley, finely chopped
- 3 scallions, finely chopped
- zest of 1 lemon
- ½ tsp pul biber, plus extra to garnish
- 5½ oz (150 g) lamb tail fat, cold
- oil, for greasing
- sea salt

Straight off the bat we're gonna need a sharp knife for this. I've treated this recipe as if I'm working with meat and prepped the fish in the same way. So, we'll be mincing the fish by hand, which is a lot easier and quicker if you have a sharp knife. Blunt knives are one of my biggest pet peeves; I'd recommend buying a basic knife and learning how to sharpen it either on a steel or a whetstone. There are loads of videos showing you how to do it on YouTube. Just give it a try and teach yourself—essentially it's all about angles, the rest of it is just making time to do it.

Finely chop the haddock and the salmon; I did them separately and then mixed them together. So, cut the fish into more manageable pieces and then cross-chop through them until they're really small chunks—the same way you'd cut a herb really fine. We want little bits of texture, not a smooth paste. Once the fish is minced, you should be able to pick it up off the board and shape it into

CONTINUES OVERLEAF

DENİZ ÇIPURASI
350.00
DENİZ LEVREĞİ
375.00
850.00
BAŞAK

a ball with no air gaps and without it falling apart; if it has gaps or bubbles, just keep chopping until it comes together. Once both fish are minced, stick them in a bowl. Cut each shrimp into about 8 pieces and add them to the mixture. Add the parsley, scallions and lemon zest. Go in with 2 big grinds of salt and the pul biber next.

Cut the fat so it's roughly the same size as the haddock and salmon and add to the mix. Gently bring the mixture together with your fingers, but don't overmix or squelch it in between your fingers, just bring it together and make sure everything is equally spread.

Using a patty shaper or cookie cutter (I used a 5 inch/13 cm one), press the mixture into the mold to make nice even fish köftes, about 2 inches (5 cm) in height, otherwise they will overcook on a really hot grill. Store them on greased parchment paper; this makes them easier to put on the grill without fucking around too much. Once shaped, leave them in the fridge to chill for a bit.

Light the BBQ and grill the köftes over a fierce 2 count (see page 246). I always give them a little touch of oil that I spread thinly with my fingers and another little grind of salt. Stick the side you've just seasoned onto the grill. Then you can peel away the paper from the other side and add another grind of salt. Grill the köftes for about 2 minutes, then give them a quarter turn—this will give you a nice burger-style crisscross pattern. Turn them and repeat the process. Each köfte should take about 4 minutes in total. Don't move them about too much, just give them a quarter turn and flip them over. I know when we're cooking something new that we as humans have an investigative nature and wanna poke and prod and be nosy, but if you do this the köftes will start to break and you'll be crushed. It happened to me and now I'm saving you the bore of having to make this mixture twice to get it right. Just trust me. Alternatively, if you wanna be super-safe and know these are gonna work first time, you can cook them in a good nonstick frying pan on the stove. It will take about the same amount of time, but I'd add a pat of butter once you've turned them.

Anyways, fish köfte are pretty damn good, to be fair. Traditionally, they'd be eaten with some good crispy bread, a raw onion, arugula and a couple of pickles, but do as you please. I'm pretty sure they'd make a pretty good fish burger, too.

EF GF

SERVES 3

When in Istanbul, you've gotta go to Kumkapı and drink rakı and eat turbot. Being on the Bosphorus, it would be a huge shame not to eat some super-fresh seafood and eat with the locals. Order a stupid amount of cold meze and a whole turbot—which is about a third of the price you can buy one for in North America. It's a proper vibe at Kumkapı: live music, fried small fish, rakı by the bottle, and I'm sure it's a part of Istanbul a lot of tourists miss. It's not somewhere you'll find on Tripadvisor; it's pretty much a place you have to know about. It's in the very bottom of Fatih.

KALKAN Kumkapı turbot

4 lb–4 lb 8 oz (1.8–2 kg) turbot, head removed, split down the middle and cut into 2 inch (5 cm) steaks (ask your fishmonger to do this for you)
sunflower or vegetable oil, for drizzling
sea salt

TO SERVE
a few lettuce leaves
1 onion, quartered
arugula
sliced lemons

The turbot in Türkiye has a tougher skin than our turbot, and the hard little bumps on their skin are huge in Türkiye, so they don't really advise you eat the skin. This means that they cook their turbot flesh-side down, which is against everything I was taught, however, it does add to the flavor, so for this recipe we're gonna cook it my way and the way the Turks do.

Get your BBQ lit, and once the charcoal is white hot, spread the coals so you have an even layer of heat at a steady 2 count (see page 246). Make sure your grill rack warms up completely before you put your fish on.

For the fish, once it's back from the fishmongers, give it a rinse under a cold tap, making sure to wash off any blood or gunk. Completely dry the fish using a clean kitchen cloth. Although turbot is quite a fatty fish, it still needs a bit of oil to get it going. Pour a small amount of oil on to each piece of fish and spread it all the way round with your hands. Season the turbot with salt.

Lay the fatter pieces of turbot, flesh-side down, on the grill, and the slimmer bits with more skin coverage, stick them skin-side down. There's not much else to do here—turbot takes a while to cook, so we're looking at about 20 minutes. Don't be tempted to poke and prod the fish—for the first 5 minutes, just let it do its thing, otherwise the fish will break if you try to move it. Then cook it for 6 minutes on each side. And then 3 minutes on each side, just to make sure it's cooked all the way through; the smaller bits that are only 2-sided with more skin on will take about 6 minutes a side and that's it.

Please rest your turbot; the juice that a turbot releases is gelatinous, meaty and almost buttery, and is super-delicious when you've squeezed some lemon over the top. To plate, lay a few leaves of lettuce on an oval plate, add all the fish, lying flat with no bits touching, throw on a few bits of onion, some arugula and the sliced lemons.

EF GF

SERVES 1

My brother isn't a fish fan and described this dish as "the juice you get at the bottom of the trash," but I thought it was delicious. This is a dish I was inspired to cook after my travels in Trabzon. It's quite a selfish one—it's basically a one-man cheater fish stew. Cooking in parchment paper has been a French thing for years, which has been adapted by many a community. I had a very similar dish in Trabzon that had cheese in but I felt like it wasn't bringing much but fat, so I swapped it out for butter and olive oil.

Go to a good fishmonger for your bit of cod, although you can use any white fish that's firm, flaky and breaks away like big fish scales. Season your cod generously with salt, and scatter over a light coating of sugar, too. Do this all over the fish and leave it to sit until you're ready to cook. This is going to help the fish firm up, draw out its moisture and also mean it doesn't need to be cooked all the way through as it gently steams in the bag.

BALIK KAĞIT KEBABI Cod in parchment

1 red pointy pepper
1 fennel bulb
olive oil, for frying
1 cap of rakı
½ white onion, finely sliced
4 black olives, pitted
4 green olives, pitted
4 cherry tomatoes, halved
1 long Turkish green pepper, deseeded and roughly chopped
good pinch of pul biber
9 oz (250 g) fillet of cod, skinned and seasoned (see intro)
1 tbsp butter
2 tbsp dry white wine
sea salt

TO SERVE
½ lemon
pinch of finely chopped flat-leaf parsley

Start off by blistering your red pepper. You can do this over a flame on your stovetop or in a really hot oven (475°F/240°C) until the flesh is soft and the skin charred. Blister the skin until it's fully charred but not crispy, with a tinge of blue. If you try to rush this process, the pepper won't let you peel it because you've been an impatient cowboy. Transfer the red pepper to a bowl, cover with plastic wrap and leave to steam. Once it's cool, peel the pepper and discard any seeds.

Take the head off the fennel, reserving any fronds for later. Cut the fennel in half and then into eighths. Get a frying pan over high heat and, once it's warm, add a splash of olive oil. Stick the fennel in with a grind of salt and cook for about 5 minutes until you get a nice brown caramelization on both sides. Add the rakı—the alcohol will vaporize and the pan will flambé. Once the flames have cooked off, add a capful of water and stick a lid on the pan just to give it a quick steam. Once all the liquid is cooked off, take the fennel off the heat. We're not looking for completely cooked and limp, as we're cooking it again in the oven.

Preheat the oven to 425°F (220°C).

Take a piece of parchment paper about 4 times the length of your cod. Working with the paper in landscape, put the onion slices down the middle first. As the onion slices are raw, we want them to take on as much heat as possible in the short cook, and they'll almost get to stew in all the juices and butter. Add the fennel and pepper next, keeping them quite tight and compact, near enough the same shape as your fish. Season every layer of food you put down with salt, not loads but as this is a dish that's coming together in a short time, we want to make sure that everything has flavor as well as being cooked properly. Add all the olives next. Then the tomatoes and green pepper. Season with the pul biber. Stick the cod on top, then add the butter and a splash of olive oil. Fold the paper in half from east to west and roll the edge, crimping it together until you get all the way round to the other side, but don't close the hole off straight away. Pour in the white wine, then seal it.

Stick the fish parcel on a baking sheet and bake for 8 minutes. Once baked, let it sit for a minute before you open it, just for the flavors to settle and so you don't burn yourself on the steam. Squeeze over the lemon, then scatter over the parsley and any reserved fennel fronds to finish.

I mean it makes sense, so why do we just focus on putting bits of meat on sticks and grilling them when we can do the same with fish, too?

I've gone for haddock and salmon here again and I'll tell you why. Salmon is a fattier fish, meaning that it will give us smoke and a good flavor, and I prefer haddock over cod. It's not as flaky and it's a denser fish, so it can hold up to intense heat. You can use any fish here really, monkfish would be great, likewise brill, halibut and turbot, but they're gonna break the bank.

For the Turkish peppers, try to use the long dark green ones but you can use the green kapyas, too, or if you really wanna go for it, use the green chiles you can find in most international supermarkets. If you can't find any of these, by all means use a regular red or green bell pepper, or don't use any veg at all. The cherry tomatoes don't need anything doing to them, just keep them whole. I wouldn't swap them for anything else—don't think "I can use a big tomato and just chop it up." It'll cook too quickly, lose all of its juice and you'll end up with nothing. Let the cherry tomatoes slowly blister and cook inside out—they go great with the peppers and fish. Trust me. Just make sure your peppers are cut to about the same length as your fish.

Also, for the love of God, don't mess around with bamboo skewers, please. Just buy some proper metal skewers—all international food stores sell 'em or they can easily be bought online, and if you look after them, they'll outlive you.

BALIK ŞİŞ Trabzon fish shish

- 5 long green Turkish peppers, each deseeded and cut into 4 pieces
- 10½ oz (300 g) haddock, skinned and chopped into 1 inch (2.5 cm) cubes
- 10½ oz (300 g) salmon, skinned and chopped into 1 inch (2.5 cm) cubes
- 20 cherry tomatoes
- olive oil, for drizzling
- sea salt

To build the skewers, I did mine like this: pepper, fish, tomato, fish, pepper, fish, tomato, pepper. When you skewer the fish, pinch it between your fingers, like you would with meat, so the flesh contracts and then skewer against the grain. This means that the fish will stay on the skewers and not roll around when you try to turn them. I also kept the fish separate, so I did a salmon skewer and a haddock skewer because the fish cook at different times and we can eat the salmon medium-rare.

Get the BBQ lit and at a good 2 count (see page 246). Oil the skewers, spreading the oil with your hands as we only want a thin layer, and season well with salt.

Cook the skewers for about 4 minutes on each side; you want the peppers and the tomatoes to blister and soften, the fish should be tense to the touch but still have a good bounce. As the salmon is naturally fattier, it will caramelize quicker and start to turn a brown color. Remember you can eat the salmon undercooked, so don't murder it—once the peppers and tomatoes are cooked,

TO SERVE
olive oil
dried flowering oregano
pul biber
lemon wedges

the salmon will be, too. A good visual cue with salmon is that the fish will start to seep a fatty white substance—that's the fat breaking down. If it's doing that all over, it's good to go.

Again, you can cook these in a frying pan but they're just not the same.

I serve the fish on the skewers—don't bother pulling it off as it will break. Let the skewers sit on a serving plate for a few minutes before giving them a good zigzag of olive oil, a little sprinkling of flowering oregano or the regular stuff (whatever you've got) and a big pinch of pul biber for color and heat. Stick a couple of lemon wedges on the plate and you're good to go.

EF GF

SERVES 4

I ate this alone in Kumkapı: a little circular set-up of Turkish men playing folk music in the distance, surrounded by stray cats, 80% bread in my stomach. As a chef, I've never really felt a type of way about eating alone, and with Türkiye having such an important food culture, it's not uncommon to just sit and chill on your own to have a second with some good food. The waiters at this restaurant snickered at the size of my order. A whole bottle of rakı, grilled squid, feta salad and a whole turbot. It's called research mate, ever heard of it?

This squid has smoky, tense meat that almost snaps back like an elastic band when you bite into it. I love the little crispy bits of flesh you get when you've scored it correctly, and the milky resting juices you get to mop up on the plate with a bit of bread. Death-row thing for me.

IZGARA KALAMAR

Grilled squid with flowering oregano and pul biber

- 1 lb 2 oz (500 g) squid, cleaned
- 2 garlic cloves, grated
- 1 tsp pul biber
- 1 tsp dried flowering oregano
- 5 tbsp olive oil
- sea salt

TO SERVE

- ½ lemon
- soy sauce (optional)

Fresh squid can look alien but, for real, it's very easy to prep. You'll have your tubes and your tentacles: the side of the tube that's open will have an uneven opening—trim it off, making sure it's cut straight, then set aside. Set the tentacles aside too.

Pick up the squid and look inside the tube: you'll see it's not totally circular—there's a little groove that runs all the way down, which is where the quill sits.

Lay the squid flat, with the groove facing away from you. Using the groove as a guideline, push your knife all the way through the squid's body, making sure the knife comes out at the tip. As you cut through the groove, the squid should open up.

Once open, there will be some gunky stuff on the inside. Use a butter knife to scrape away any snotty bits on both sides. Repeat this process on all the tubes, then wash them thoroughly in a colander, along with the tentacles.

Place the squid on a chopping board, with the inside of the tube facing you. You'll know it's the inside because its softer in texture and not as solid in color. At a 45-degree angle, score the flesh of the squid into little diamond shapes. This gives the dressing a chance to sit in those little grooves.

CONTINUES OVERLEAF

In order for our marinade to cling, the squid has to be dry. Cut the squid into 3 equal pieces, then pat them dry with a clean, dry cloth. Leave them to lie on top of the cloth for 5 minutes or so, to absorb any remaining moisture.

Stick the squid in a bowl, then add the garlic, pul biber, oregano and olive oil before mixing well. Squid doesn't really need too long to marinate, it's more an exterior flavoring, so you can either do this 5 minutes or a couple of hours before cooking—it's totally up to you.

Now by all means, fry this in a frying pan BUT you'd be missing a trick if you didn't BBQ it. One of my favorite recipes from my first book, HOME, is the grilled squid and smashed tomatoes. There's something special about charcoal and squid: the smoke, the speed it cooks, the sweetness in the smell, the way the squid wriggles under intense heat... The squid basically guides you through the cooking process—you've just gotta know what to look for.

Once the BBQ is up to a 1 count (see "How to Light a BBQ" on page 246), season the marinated squid with salt. Once you think you've seasoned it properly, add another little extra for me.

Stick the tentacles on the grill first, as they'll need slightly more time to cook, and I like them a little crispy. Once the legs start to spread and crisp, place on the rest of your squid, scored-side down. Let it do its thing for 3–4 minutes and don't touch it.

Where the squid is scored, you'll see that the lines you've sliced in become more visible as the flesh starts to turn from translucent to a solid block white, which is a signal that it's time to turn. Using a pair of tongs, pick up the squid. Instinctively, it will want to coil. Grill the coiled squid for another minute or so, to get nice crispy edges.

Place the squid on a serving plate, along with half a lemon that's ready for squeezing. When I ate this in Türkiye, it was served with a little pot of soy sauce, which isn't traditional—but it works.

04

VEG

TRABZON (Northeastern Türkiye)

I'm staying in the hills of Trabzon, on the steepest road I've ever seen in my life. It may as well be a theme park roller coaster. It's a cold, foggy March night, and as the cab man drove me here, weaving round hilly roads, his prayer beads swung from side to side on the dashboard. When I got to the hotel, I had just missed dinner service. Not having done any research on where to eat, I hail another cab and ask the driver to take me to the closest grocery store in the hope of getting some bits to make, what I call, The Touchdown Sandwich. Arriving anywhere abroad, I always do the same thing: loaf of bread, stumpy cucumbers, proper tomatoes and a hunk of local cheese, with a side of ketchup-flavored potato chips and a foreign cola. Being in Trabzon means there's a fridge full of homemade cheeses—I get *eski kaşar*, which is like a Turkish, aged mozzarella. I buy the cab man a loaf of bread and some cheese to say thank you for waiting for me. Considering the cab fare was only $5, I thought I'd hook him up as well. He tells me about all the places I should eat, then slips me his card and tells me if I ever need him, he's there.

Trabzon is a bit of a sleepy city—it's cold and everyone is minding their own business. It feels like an older city, like the average age could have been forty. Men wearing suits for no reason in Türkiye is a thing; not a work thing, but just a style thing. Old Turkish men are almost always clean shaven around a slug mustache, wearing some sort of blazer—and Trabzon men are no different. There isn't much color here—under the grey sky, everyone's wearing black. Men link arms in quilted jet-black puffers, head-scarved ladies blend in like camouflage, swiftly moving in and out of grocery stores like it's a police sting op. The only color around is the Trabzonspor soccer colors: maroon, blue and white. I'm not kidding, it's like I've ended up at a Burnley F.C. away game. Red tiled walls and pastel blue European buildings that are tall and skinny surround the square.

Trabzon doesn't have the same fast pace of I-need-to-be-moving-at-100mph-Istanbul. People sit here, chill, feed stray dogs, smoke cigs and watch the day go by. I get stopped in the square by an elderly man with a walking stick. His teeth have been filed into little tic tac shapes—he's obviously still on the waiting list for the Türkiye-teeth glow up. 'I've been watching you from afar," he says. Here it comes: something that's gonna be terribly rude and probably make me feel shit for the rest of the day. "I couldn't help but notice your eyelashes!"—Nah, he didn't really say that, but it would have been fucking funny if he did. He actually said, "I think you might be the tallest man I've seen, and if it wasn't for that thing in your hand, you'd be even taller," kindly referencing my Camel Yellow cigarette.

Turks can be, and will be, outspoken, abrupt and not conscious of the power of words. I'm used to it. My dad used to sport me and my brother Arif around like prized cattle. Kamil loved people saying, 'Oh Kamil, your sons are so tall and solid!." Fuck knows why, maybe it's a pride thing where he thinks he has super-sperm that's produced two sons who are 'strong like stone," as he would say. I'm not that easily offended, but there's times I can't be bothered to hear it. Imagine if you, the reader of this book, had a massive nose—like *freakishly* long, hooked or crooked. Imagine if every day I popped up in your bathroom, behind your shower curtain, to remind you how big it was. That's how I sometimes feel about being called big. I know how to deal with it more now—sometimes I'm just like "Yeah mate, thanks," but other times, if you catch me on a bad day, I can make a snide remark. My favorite will always be "Well, I've done shits bigger than you" with a little I'll-still-fuck-you-up chuckle.

Although Trabzon has the same atmosphere as a wake, the food doesn't disappoint: breakfast cheese pides, fish sis and köfte from down the road in Akçaabat, everything drowned in butter, breakfasts of kuymak and plenty of bread ... this is my introduction to food I've never seen before in Türkiye. I want to know where the ingredients came from and how this dish originated. I feel like that's a thing we miss in the UK; we have a few select places that specialize in a breed of cow, or

a particular sandwich or what have you, but we don't really have food-led destination vacatios. No one's going to Southampton for X or driving up to Birmingham for Y. However, in Türkiye, each city, even these little villages, want to be known for something in the culinary sense. Shop windows in Trabzon have painted glass signs reading "*meşhur,*" the word for "famous." These little restaurants are celebrities in their own way, the right way, celebrated for their dedication to their craft day in and day out, producing food to the highest standard. It's about being known for one thing and doing it right. I only recently learnt that the word *sensei* doesn't just relate to Japanese dojos; the word actually means "to have spent 100,000 hours honing your craft." It's about dedicating your life to something at the very highest standard. For some it's mundane, producing the same thing every day for 20 years. I remember Marco Pierre White talking about how the challenge of reaching three Michelin stars was the exciting part, but maintaining them was the worst time of his life: repeating the same thing and staying at the highest standard. I think a lot of that attitude stems from the privileged speed the first world moves at. Money men are always gonna reach big heights faster—but there's no real respect in that kind of food.

Money talks in the west, but there's a common level of respect for food in Türkiye. There are hardly any takeout spots outside of the big cities; the locals just don't fuck with them. Yes, that has a lot to do with wages and income—but I also feel like everyone has the time to slow down for food here. Mealtimes are the most important part of the day, no matter what time it is. In most Turkish households, enough food is made for the people who are eating, plus accounting for any mystery guests who might turn up and socialize. That means there's always the probability of leaving the house with a Tupperware for lunch. There's a lot more of these cultural etiquettes when it comes to Türkiye: taking your fucking shoes off being number one. Never accept food straight away when offered in someone's house—always wait for the second offer. Never go to a married woman's house when her husband isn't home. But always help an elderly woman (this doesn't apply to young women, though. Sorry ladies. The whole world isn't woke yet, it's a slow movement but it'll happen).

SERVES 2

In my biased opinion, if there's one thing that the Turks do better than anyone else in the world, it's breakfast. Turkish breakfast is basically an assault course of food. Just when you think it's over, there's more. I enjoy eating Turkish breakfast out because of the way it's served; a Turkish breakfast for one is served on a plate that looks like something that would be given to you on a flight. Loads of little compartments filled with something even more delicious every time. We used to have Turkish breakfast at mine most Sundays as kids. One of us would be dragged to Yaşar Halim in Green Lanes (normally me) and would have to endure Kamil talking to almost everyone in the shop, only for him to ignore anything we actually wanted to buy.

KAHVALTI Turkish breakfast

Now this is half recipe and half "how to." You can swap out or keep whatever you want. Change the eggs, get your favorite bread. But I'd recommend making the butter (see page 24) and getting some tea going (see page 216).

There's always a white cheese like a feta involved, or kaşar peyniri, which are big yellow wheels of cheese in Turkish stores—an all-rounder, non-invasive, like a huge Babybel for adults. The last cheese is always a regional cheese, sometimes it's dil peyniri in long thin strands, or a blue if you're in Adana.

Also, you want a little plate of "salad" for crunch. A couple of stumpy cucumbers and a nice tomato—beef, cherry or a special one from a deli. None of that watery cheap supermarket stuff. Peel the cucumbers in alternate sections, leaving several strips of skin so you're left with a pattern that resembles zebra print. I normally stick a few long dark green peppers and black olives on that plate, too.

Same with bread, use whatever you want; Turks will have Ramazan pidesi (see page 154) with breakfast or a sandwich loaf.

As if all of that wasn't enough, you need a sweet section—jams are a must, use them like you would a chutney on a cheese board; also stick a bit of Nutella on a plate with pistachios. Legit.

There's normally some sort of fried element in a Turkish breakfast and it's usually a sigara böreği, which is the easiest of börek. When you're picking up filo pastry in an international supermarket, you'll notice it comes in all different shapes and sizes. For sigara böreği, you're gonna need the filo that's already cut into triangles; if you can't get this, we all did elementary school math, so you'll figure it out.

SIGARA BÖREĞI Rolled cheese fingers

7 oz (200 g) beyaz peynir
¼ bunch of flat-leaf parsley, roughly chopped
any type of oil, for frying
8 sheets of store-bought filo pastry
black pepper

Crumble the beyaz peynir into little bits in your hands. Mix in the parsley and some black pepper.

Pour enough oil into a frying pan to shallow-fry the böreks, about 1 inch (2.5 cm) will do, and heat it to about 340°F (170°C). Check using a thermometer.

The store-bought filo will be cut into pizza slices. Spoon a tablespoon and a bit of the filling on to the wider side of the filo, keeping a ½ inch (1 cm) gap from the sides. Roll up the filo once so that you start to make a sausage shape, then close off the open sides of the filo. Tuck in the sides nice and tight to make sure nothing spills out. Repeat with the remaining filo and filling—you should have 8 böreks in total.

Fry the böreks for 5 minutes until golden on both sides. The filling isn't gonna melt in the middle, so we're just looking for the filo to crisp. Drain the böreks on a piece of paper towel and serve.

SERVES 2

Kuymak is from Trabzon, the dairy part of Türkiye, where the cheese and butter are from up in the hills. It's a breakfast dish made with polenta, butter and loads of stringy cheese. It's not one of those you order on your own, but it's a great little breakfast sharer. Get the tea on.

KUYMAK Breakfast cheese and polenta

- 5 tbsp (70 g) butter
- ⅔ cup (100 g) fine polenta
- 1¼ cups (300 ml) warm water
- 3½ oz (100 g) dil peyniri Turkish string cheese, washed 3 times to draw out the salt, then drained
- 9 oz (250 g) kaşar peyniri, grated
- 2½ oz (70 g) strong Cheddar, grated
- 2 tbsp milk
- sea salt

Traditionally, Turks would make this in a copper pan because they retain the heat better, but if you don't have one, a normal frying pan will work, preferably not one with huge sides.

Melt the butter over medium heat but don't let it color. Once the butter has melted and is starting to bubble, add the polenta and a big pinch of salt. Fry the polenta for a couple minutes until it's a light caramel color and you can smell it starting to toast. Add half the water and bring it to a boil but keep stirring it—the water will absorb into the polenta very quickly. Add the remaining water and keep it moving and cooking for about 4 minutes. Gently cook the polenta for 10 minutes until the grains are soft.

Once the polenta grains are soft, drop the heat to low and add all the cheeses and the milk. Don't season it yet. Stir in the cheeses until they're completely melted—you should have a really stringy cheese mixture that you can wrap around the spoon and pull up from the pan quite high. Taste the mixture to see if it needs any more salt—the white stringy Turkish cheese is quite salty anyway. Serve with loads of bread and Turkish tea.

ÖZ NEHİR
LUX
ELOXAL

SERVES 2

*Many men

"*Menemen** wish death upon me. Blood in my eye, dawg, and I can't see. I'm tryin' to be what I'm destined to be ..."—"Many Men" (2003), 50 Cent.

This is an absolute classic Turkish breakfast dish. Türkiye is very much divided when it comes to making menemen: the biggest controversy is whether it's made with or without onions. Some people add cheese, some add sausage, garlic and cumin. I'm giving you my version; the way I think it should be eaten.

One of the most common mistakes that people make when making menemen is not getting the egg ratio right. If you make menemen using the whole egg, it makes the mixture snotty and wet due to the liquid in the egg white. To avoid this, we're going to make a richer egg mixture by adding a couple of extra egg yolks. I find rich yolks have a bigger flavor; great for pastas and baking.

MENEMEN Tomato and pepper scrambled eggs

- 14 oz (400 g) white onions, finely diced
- 2 tbsp olive oil
- 10½ oz (300 g) beefsteak tomatoes
- 7 oz (200 g) cherry tomatoes
- 3½ oz (100 g) sivri peppers (about 4), deseeded and finely diced
- 2 eggs, plus 4 egg yolks
- 1¾ oz (50 g) Kaşkaval cheese, grated
- ¼ oz (10 g) sucuk (Turkish breakfast sausage), sliced
- ½ oz (15 g) butter
- sea salt
- warm rustic bread, to serve

In a large frying pan over low-medium heat, fry the onions in the olive oil with a big grind of salt until they are soft and translucent. Meanwhile, blanch the beefsteak tomatoes and cherry tomatoes in boiling water for 1–1½ minutes, which will make peeling their skins much easier.

Chop the beefsteak and cherry tomatoes and set aside in separate piles. The beefsteak tomatoes will be our base flavor and cherry tomatoes will lend sweetness.

Once the onions have sweated down, stir in the peppers. We only want to fry them for a couple of minutes so that they still have bite. Add all the chopped beefsteak tomatoes plus half of the chopped cherry tomatoes to the pan and stir. Add a big grind of salt and leave over medium heat for the moisture to cook out. Once the tomato liquid has evaporated, the mixture will be dry enough to start frying again. You'll hear the difference in the tomatoes; they will change from a simmering *blip blip blip* to a frying *hisssssss.*

Whisk together the eggs and the egg yolks, then swirl them into the pan. Add a grind of salt to season, then gently stir for about a minute over medium heat to combine with the onion mixture. While the eggs are still runny, pour in the remaining chopped cherry tomatoes and leave the mixture to cook.

As soon as the eggs have cooked and look like a loose omelet, transfer the mixture to an ovenproof dish. Top generously with the cheese and sucuk, then place under a hot grill until the cheese melts and the sucuk is warm. Add the butter to the top of the dish, then you're ready to eat.

GF V

SERVES 2

The eggs of a Turkish breakfast change wherever you go in Türkiye, but mostly you get served a semi-mixed, crispy-bottomed omelet, cooked in loads of foaming butter.

OMLET Turkish omelet

3 tbsp butter
4 eggs
sea salt

You need a good nonstick pan for this. I only ever buy free-range eggs with rich yolks, not because I'm a snob, but I just believe in the ethos of free-range and they taste better.

Heat a frying pan over medium heat, add in 2 tablespoons of the butter and gently melt it. When the butter slowly starts to foam, crack in the eggs and break the yolks. Season the eggs with a good pinch of salt.

Give the eggs a quick mix with a spatula, making sure you're scraping the bottom of the pan. Once you've got a marbled effect, crank up the heat to high.

No more moving or stirring, let the eggs fry hard on one side for about a minute.

Scatter over the remaining butter and cover the eggs with a lid.

Turn off the heat and let the eggs sit for a minute before serving.

Seğmen
GELENEKSEL
KAYISI REÇELİ
TAMEK

Nutkum
PEKMEZ

SERVES 6

The soup game is a huge thing in Türkiye, with each region having its own celebrated soup: Beyran çorbası (spicy lamb and rice soup) in Gaziantep, yayla çorbası from the meadows in the north, or kelle paça (made from sheeps' heads) in Adana. However, one soup that brings Türkiye together as a nation is red lentil soup. No matter where you go, you'll always find it on a menu. It does vary from place to place; some serve it runny, while others add potatoes to help it thicken. I like mine on the thicker side. Use a good stock for this soup to get the full flavor—if you can't be bothered to make one of mine (see pages 26 and 27), buy the bagged or canned stuff in the supermarkets.

MERCIMEK ÇORBASI Red lentil soup

- 1 lb 2 oz (500 g) dried split red lentils
- any type of oil, for frying
- 6 carrots, peeled and finely diced
- 3 large onions, finely diced
- 3 garlic cloves, cracked and peeled
- 2 tbsp pul biber, plus extra to serve
- 1 tbsp cumin seeds
- 1 heaped tbsp aci biber salçasi
- 12½ cups (3 liters) vegetable stock or water
- 3 medium potatoes, peeled and diced
- sea salt and pepper
- pat of butter (see page 24 for homemade), to serve

To prep the lentils, rinse them under cold water until the water runs clear. Soak the lentils in fresh water for at least 30 minutes.

Start off by sticking a big pot over medium heat and adding enough oil to cover the bottom. Allow the oil to come up to smoking point and add your carrots. We're adding our carrots first to draw out all the sugars. Cook the carrots for 20 minutes, just until the edges start to brown. Add the onions next, along with 2 big grinds of salt. The onions will need to cook down until they're soft and translucent. Chuck in the whole garlic cloves, then add the pul biber and cumin seeds and fry for a couple of minutes until fragrant.

Add the pepper paste and let it fry for about 5 minutes, changing the color of the oil to a nice bronze. Add the washed and drained lentils, giving them a good stir to get coated in the base. I cook the lentils dry like this until all the remaining water on them has evaporated—you'll be able to hear the change when the water has fully cooked off and the lentils begin to fry. Once frying, cover the lentils with the stock. Bring to a boil and then drop in the potatoes. The potatoes aren't really there for flavor but more to help the soup thicken.

Simmer the soup for 35–45 minutes until the lentils and potatoes are cooked all the way through. Blend the soup with a stick blender or in a Nutribullet, whatever you've got. Blend the soup until it's nice and smooth. Season again with loads of salt and freshly cracked black pepper.

Pour the soup into a large serving bowl. Normally mercimek çorbası has a little pul biber melted butter over the top, but I just cut in a pat of homemade butter and cover it in pul biber.

If you're eating mercimek çorbası in Türkiye, it's always served with a huge plate of fresh bread, raw turnips, arugula, raw onions and black olives.

EF GF

SERVES 4

Traditionally eaten for Ramadan, this is more than just a rice dish. It's a celebratory dish that normally has lamb in it, but I've decided to go lamb-less so that it's easy and you can make it whenever you want. I picked this up from a restaurant serving food specific to Konya in Türkiye. Rice with pine nuts, almonds, raisins full of butter. Served alongside stewed meats, or fresh salads, eat it with whatever you want. Also, it's a good little party dish to whip up if you're ever invited to a baby shower or funeral.

For this recipe, you're gonna need to get yourself some baldo rice—short little fat stubby grains—found in most supermarkets. I guess you can make this with any rice you want, as long as you know how to cook it. The idea is that we're just flavoring the rice and making it more special than it already is. I'm a huge snob when it comes to cooking the basics, getting baked potatoes right, cooking pasta perfectly and rice being individual grains, seasoned and not clumpy. I don't trust people who claim they can cook rice and then can't.

MEVLEVI PILAVI Rice with carrots, pine nuts and walnuts

- 1 mug of baldo (or white basmati) rice
- any type of oil, for frying
- 3 onions, roughly chopped
- ¾ cup (100 g) pine nuts
- ¾ cup (100 g) almonds
- 3 tbsp raisins
- 4 medium carrots, peeled and diced
- 5 tbsp (75 g) butter
- 2 cinnamon sticks
- pinch of ground allspice
- 1 tsp sugar
- chicken or vegetable stock (see page 26 for homemade)
- salt and pepper

Whatever mug you use to measure the rice with, that's the same mug you use for the water. That's the first basic step to getting rice right. Measure out a mug of rice—a normal mug, a little mug, a novelty rather rude mug you got as a secret Santa gift. Soak the rice in cold water for 1 hour, making sure the rice is fully covered in water. This will help cook the rice and make sure all the grains are cooked uniformly.

Once the rice is soaked, drain the water and rinse the rice in a sieve with small holes until the water runs fully clear. I don't wash chickens, but you'll never catch me cooking unwashed rice man, over my dead body. People break their backs planting and harvesting that shit, so you've gotta pay it respect.

Once the water is running completely clear, allow the rice to drain and get on with the flavors.

In a high-sided pot over medium heat, add enough oil to coat the base of the pot. We just want oil to get the onions cooking, as I don't like to slowly sweat onions in butter; if the pan gets too hot, you'll get too much color too quickly, or the butter can brown. There's just too many factors for a possible fuck-up, so stick to oil for the beginning.

CONTINUES OVERLEAF

Add your onions with a big grind of salt and cook them slowly for about 20 minutes until they're soft and translucent. We really want to build a sweetness in the background for this rice and this is going to come from onions and carrots. Both these vegetables have a high sugar content and we want to slowly bring that sweetness out to add loads of flavor to our rice.

While the onions are softening, there's a couple of bits we need to do at the same time in a separate pan.

Stick a dry frying pan over low heat and gently toast the pine nuts and the almonds. We don't need like a caramel color all the way round, just a light toast until they're nice and warm. Also soak the raisins in enough boiling water to cover for at least 3 minutes.

Back to the rice. Once the onions are soft, sweet and translucent, add the carrots and cook for a further 5 minutes, just to take the raw edge off them.

Go in with the butter next and allow it to melt and begin to fry. Add the spices, nuts, drained raisins, sugar and some seasoning. Then add the rice and fry for a couple of minutes. Cover the rice with enough stock to come up to your first finger. Stir the liquid into the rice and bring it to a boil. Taste the liquid and make sure it's seasoned enough. You want to be able to taste the salt.

Once the rice is boiling, stir the mixture until the liquid is almost fully absorbed. Lay a clean tea towel over the rice, put a lid on top and stick it over the lowest heat. Steam for 10 minutes. It's important that you don't lift the lid on the rice at this point and just trust the process. Once the 10 minutes is up, turn off the heat and allow the rice to steam for 15–20 minutes.

Done.

EF GF

SERVES 4

There are loads of variations of eggplant dishes in Turkish cuisine, but this is possibly the easiest. Now although this recipe is in the vegetable chapter and contains meat, this dish is more of a celebration of the eggplant itself. A great mid-week recipe with rice and a good salad, and a proper Turkish household staple. You do really need the long, skinnier eggplants for this dish, as they're sweeter and don't take anywhere near as long to cook.

KARNIYARIK Stuffed eggplants

- 2 lb 4 oz (1 kg) long, skinny eggplants (about 8 in total)
- any type of oil, for frying the eggplants
- olive oil, for frying
- 2 lb 4 oz (1 kg) ground beef
- 1 lb 10 oz (750 g) white onions, finely diced
- 4 kapya peppers
- 4 garlic cloves, thinly sliced
- 1 tbsp pul biber
- 2 tbsp tomato paste
- 1 lb 6 oz (630 g) tomatoes, grated
- pinch of sugar
- salt and pepper

To start, peel the eggplants in alternate sections, leaving several strips of skin ½ inch (1 cm) wide. You should be left with a pattern that resembles zebra print.

Then salt them heavily and leave them to sit for at least 30 minutes to draw out the moisture. The reason we do this is so we can get a solid fry on the eggplants—we want them crispy and golden, not light and floppy.

Half-fill a deep, heavy-based frying pan with oil and stick it over medium heat until the oil reaches at least 340°F (170°C). Use a thermometer for this. It's super-important that the oil is at the right temperature, otherwise the eggplants will fill with oil and become heavy and not caramelize and gain any flavor.

While the oil is heating up, let's get going with the filling. Set the biggest frying pan you've got over high heat with a good drizzle of olive oil and get it smoking hot. Add the ground beef and break it down with the back of a spoon. The beef will cook in stages—it'll begin to color as soon as it hits the pan, but as it starts to come up to temperature, it'll begin to release liquid. Cook off all this liquid until it's completely evaporated and the meat begins to fry again. Fry the beef until it's crispy and a deep brown color, then add the onions and a big grind of salt. Turn down to a medium heat and fry the onions for a good 15–20 minutes until they're soft, sweet and have taken on the color in the pan. Don't rush this—cook the onions to bring out as much flavor as possible.

Add the eggplants to the hot oil, not all at once, a couple of batches will do. Fry for 6–8 minutes until they're completely soft and a nice dark brown in color. Once all the eggplants are cooked, let them rest on some paper towels to suck up any unwanted oil.

CONTINUES OVERLEAF

In the same oil as you used to cook the eggplants, fry off the peppers. They won't take long at all—just fry them until the skin starts to blister and peel. Stick them with the eggplants to drain.

Once the onions are cooked, add the garlic and fry for about 4 minutes. Season heavily with salt and pepper, then give it a taste to see if it needs any more salt. Add the pul biber and 1 tablespoon of the tomato paste and stir that in. Let the tomato paste coat everything in the pan and fry for a couple of minutes. Add the grated tomatoes and half a mug of boiling water, then bring to a boil. Sprinkle in the sugar and let it blip for a couple of minutes. Don't cook the moisture out of the mixture completely—it should resemble a bolognese.

Peel any loose skin off the peppers, cut them open and get rid of any seeds. Try to keep the peppers all in one piece, as it makes them easier to stuff. Break the eggplants in half lengthways and give the flesh a little grind of salt. Stuff the eggplants and peppers with the beef mixture until you've run out. I do this in a roasting pan, laying them all out with enough space in between for them to cook; you might need to use 2 trays depending on the size of the eggplants.

Preheat the oven to 400°F (200°C).

Make a little sauce by mixing the remaining tablespoon of tomato paste into a large mug of boiling water until the tomato paste has melted. Pour that into the gaps between the eggplants and peppers—I didn't pour it directly into the mix, just around. Bake for about 30 minutes until the sauce has cooked off and some bits of beef have caught and gone crispy, then dig in.

Traditional mücver are just zucchini and dill fritters—a dish that dates as far back as the Ottoman Empire. Yeah, they're great when they're done right, but often they can be a little limp and drowned in oil. I like fritters on the lighter side, packed with herbs. I added corn to these for a little extra texture and sweetness and it worked a treat.

PEYNIRLI MÜCVER Zucchini, feta and corn fritters

4 zucchinis
½ bunch of cilantro, finely chopped
½ bunch of chives, finely sliced
5 scallions, finely sliced
1 cup (170 g) corn kernels
2 big pinches of pul biber
big pinch of black pepper
7 oz (200 g) feta, crumbled
2 eggs
6 heaped tbsp all-purpose flour
3 heaped tbsp cornstarch
any type of oil, for frying
salt
lemon wedge, to serve
garlic yogurt (optional), to serve

Start off by grating the zucchinis on the bigger side of a box grater; don't bother peeling the skins. Salt them heavily, mix and allow them to release all their excess water. After about 10 minutes, put the zucchinis in a clean tea towel and squeeze out all the moisture until they're bone dry.

In another bowl, add the herbs, scallions, corn, pul biber, black pepper, feta, eggs and both flours. Add the squeezed-out zucchinis and give it all a good mix. The batter should be thick and holding everything together.

Heat about ½ inch (1 cm) of oil in a wide frying pan, enough just to shallow-fry the fritters. By all means deep-fry them if you want, but you'll have more control shallow-frying them, as the longer process and lower temperature mean that the flour and cornstarch can cook out.

Spoon about 1 tablespoon of the mixture (for each fritter) into the frying pan and shallow-fry the fritters over medium heat for about 4 minutes on each side until golden and crispy. Please don't try to do them all at once. Make sure you leave enough space between the fritters, otherwise they won't crisp up and will retain all the oil.

Remove the fritters from the oil and let them rest on some paper towels to remove the excess grease. Serve warm with a lemon wedge and some garlic yogurt, if you like.

SERVES 3

Any of you that have been to Istanbul will have definitely seen or eaten corn on the cob on the streets, grilled gently and served simply with salt, normally around the tourist attractions. It's a very cheap street food, enjoyed by everyone. When I was out in Istanbul, every night I'd go to Eminönü and feed the three stray dogs I befriended. I'd get them chicken döners or köftes from the kebap boys and myself a corn on the cob. This one's for my dog that I didn't name. Side note: when I was in Istanbul six months later, I found the dog, he recognized me and sat next to me briefly while I fed him a köfte. Miss you, boy.

KÖZLENMIŞ SÜT MISIR Grilled street corn

- 3 corn on the cob, leaves and silks removed
- 5½ cups (1.3 liters) milk
- 2 tsp sugar
- salt

This one's super easy and a great little recipe for the summer. All you gotta do is stick 3 cleaned corn on the cob in a pot with the milk, sugar and a good grind or 2 of salt, then bring it to a boil. Simmer for 6 minutes. Drain the corn (discard the milk) and then they're ready to be grilled.

Grill them gently over a 3 count BBQ (see page 246), turning them every so often for 6 minutes until they start to pop and char. When we were kids, in the summer Kamil would always end a BBQ with a round of corn on the cob and eat them like a machine.

KÖZ
MISIR
40 TL
BOĞAZ TURU
ADALAR
adidas
İYOTLU
SOFRA TUZU
BİLLUR
TUZ

I had this in Gaziantep as a complementary appetizer to a kebap I ordered. Sweet, spicy and one of those dishes I believe tastes better cold. Sarma, or dolma as us Cypriots call it, is a celebration dish for family get-togethers. It's feeding all your loved ones on an unknowingly tight budget. I kept these as a vegan option because I kind of just want to celebrate the fact that we're using simple ingredients and making something delicious.

If you're not familiar with sarma or dolma, it's normally some sort of vegetable stuffed with meat and rice. I don't know the actual origins, but it defo strikes me as a dish that would have been cooked during hard times, when meat is scarce and most people already had rice, herbs and tomatoes knocking around anyway. I grew up eating dolma with huge spoonfuls of yogurt on the side and sharp acidic salads packed with parsley and good tomatoes. This recipe will make a lot of dolma—I'd say enough for at least six people. However, it makes a great packed lunch the next day, and also just live how the Turks live—leftovers don't mean you have to remake something out of them. Serve them again as a side, eat them out the fridge cold, stop being so privileged.

If the length of this recipe scares you a little, then let me break it down for you: once you've stuffed the onions, you're basically cooking rice. Can you cook rice? Yes? Then you're fine, trust me.

SOĞAN DOLMASI Stuffed onions

4 lb 8 oz (2 kg) onions
1 mug of short-grain rice, such as sushi rice
14 oz (400 g) shallots, finely diced
olive oil, for frying
2 beefsteak tomatoes
5 tbsp pomegranate molasses
¼ oz (7 g) mint, finely chopped
1 oz (25 g) parsley, finely chopped
1 tbsp pul biber
salt and pepper

Start off by peeling the onions, making sure to get rid of the outer skin. It's just a bit shitty and doesn't really cook down. Cut the onions from the top down, about halfway into the core, but not all the way through. Opening them halfway now helps with peeling them later on. Bring a large pot of water to a boil with plenty of salt, like you're cooking pasta, add the onions and boil them for about 5 minutes. We're not looking to cook the onions; we're just ensuring that they peel away and they've got a little more give so we can roll them up. Once the onions are boiled, carefully separate them layer by layer, a break here and there isn't the end of the world but you want to keep them whole if possible. Let the onions cool and crack on with the rice.

Firstly, and most importantly, wash the rice. As in a few of the dishes in this book, I used Japanese sushi rice. It's not far off from what the Turks would use. Traditionally, dolma would be cooked with baldo or short-grain, for density. Wash the rice until the water runs clear; this will take about 5 runs of water and a gentle massage to make it happen. Once washed, soak the rice in plenty of fresh water for at least 30 minutes, then drain.

FOR THE SAUCE
any type of oil, for frying
10 cherry tomatoes
5 garlic cloves, crushed
1 tbsp tomato paste
1 tsp sugar

TO SERVE (OPTIONAL)
yogurt
pul biber

Get the shallots frying gently in a generous amount of olive oil and a good grind of salt—we want to slowly caramelize the shallots to give the dolma depth.

In a bowl, grate the tomatoes, then add the pomegranate molasses, mint, parsley, caramelized shallots, soaked rice, some salt and pepper, the pul biber and olive oil. Give it all a good mix and set aside.

Take 1 teaspoon of the rice mixture and stick it into half a blanched onion, then roll the edge of the onion back on itself and continue to roll until the onion is completely wrapped around the rice. Have you ever rolled a spliff? If you have, use that technique and if you haven't, well then there's always time to start. Continue this process until you're out of rice mixture or onions. If you run out of onions, you can always blanch more but there really isn't any point in doing a dolma for one. As traditionally, in my family, dolma were made by loads of people. I have memories of my mom helping my nan and aunties stuff little vine leaves like a Cypriot sweatshop, so if you can get someone to help, then bring them in.

To make the sauce, add enough oil to coat the base of a large, heavy-based pot, and before the oil gets too hot, add the cherry tomatoes and blister all over. Add the garlic next and let it fry for about a minute—don't get loads of color on it, a little golden is fine but nothing more than that. Then add the tomato paste and fry that for a minute or so, then add a good grind of salt and the sugar. Now, using the same mug you measured the rice with, add ¾ of a mug of water and turn off the heat—don't reduce it, just stir the water through.

Place the stuffed onions in a high-sided pot, in a circular pattern, covering the entire base of the pot. Keep going until you run out of stuffed onions. Pour the tomato sauce over the onions and stick the heat on medium. Taste the sauce for seasoning, you want to be able to taste salt, not like the sea but it should be present. Put a plate on top of the onions to stop them floating about, cover the pot with a lid and bring it to a boil. Once boiling, drop the heat to low and simmer for at least 40 minutes. Once all the liquid has evaporated, remove from the heat and let the dolma chill for a bit and they'll seize a little. Stick 'em on a plate with a dollop of yogurt and some pul biber, if you like.

Böreks and all things filo are a massive thing in Türkiye. They're pick-up-and-go snacks, often served with breakfast. When I was in Adana, I was told a good few times that I had to eat cheese börek here, as unlike most böreks that are baked, this is all done on the gas burner. Cheese böreks in Adana are almost like a lasagne without the red sauce. Super-delicious, super-cheesy, with a good crunch from the filo and served with a couple of olives.

To make good börek, you need aluminum baking pans, nothing heavy, something a little bit shitty and lightweight to retain the heat and color the bottom side. You can get these easily online. Don't get a huge one, about 12 inches (30 cm) is enough for about six portions. You're also gonna need two baking pans for this recipe, but they'll come in handy for other things, too. I prefer working with rectangular ones, as it's easier to cut the filo to the right size. With circular ones, if you pack them too much, the böreks become too dense and don't cook. If you can't get either of the cheeses listed below, use a mixture of other melty cheeses, such as mozzarella and Gouda.

ADANA BÖREK Cheese-filled filo

- 17 large sheets of filo pastry (see page 23 for homemade)
- 14 tbsp (200 g) butter, plus extra for greasing
- 1⅔ cups (400 ml) milk
- 2 eggs

FOR THE FILLING

- 5½ oz (150 g) tel (çeçil) peyniri, pulled apart into strings and soaked in warm water, then drained
- 6 oz (170 g) kaşar peyniri, grated

When I say 17 sheets of filo, I know that sounds like a lot, but it's probably only 1 package of the store-bought stuff. The filo sheets in those packages are rolled on top of each other, so when you open the packages you'll get it. Cut 17 sheets of the filo to fit the baking sheet you're using (see intro) but don't throw away the trim.

Melt the butter and stick it in a bowl with a pastry brush—that's a chef word for a small paintbrush. Combine the milk and eggs in a separate bowl.

Brush the baking pan with a good coating of butter, making sure you go up the sides, too, then add the first layer of filo and brush butter all over that, too. You'll know when it's enough butter because the filo will become more see-through than before. Repeat until you've got 8 layers of filo in your pan. Using about half the trim from the filo, dip it into the milk and egg mixture and let it sit for about 5 seconds. Lift the filo out and let it drain for a second, then gently lay it on the filo—it doesn't have to be flat, so don't pack it in but just drape it until you're about halfway up the pan. Don't put all the trim in the wet mixture; do it little by little, taking your time with it. Air pockets here don't matter—an uneven börek is a better börek, as it's lighter and cooks better. Add both your cheeses. Repeat draping the scraps over the cheese just until you nearly reach the top. Then repeat the buttered layering with the remaining 9 sheets of filo.

Stick the pan over low heat on the stovetop and cook the base of the börek—you're gonna have to move the pan around to distribute the heat evenly. Move the

pan often and don't let it sit in one place for too long. Once the mixture is starting to bubble up the sides and you can smell the filo starting to crisp, here's where the second baking pan comes in. Grease that pan heavily with butter and carefully flip the pans so the base is now at the top and the raw side is on the bottom. Cook the börek for another 15 minutes.

Meanwhile, preheat the oven to 375°F (190°C).

Finish the börek in the oven for 15 minutes. Once cooked, portion up the börek and eat it hot so you get all that molten cheese. Good enough to eat on its own, but I like to eat it with something crunchy like cucumber, red pepper or some pickles. No recipe for that. Just one bite of börek, one bite of something else.

05

BREAD

DIYARBAKIR (Southeastern Türkiye)

I've given up on Trabzon after three days full of cheese, bread and grey skies, and have booked a short flight to Diyarbakır, southeastern Türkiye. It's the land of Antep, gold and silver filigree work and liver kebaps. I'm looking forward to a change of scenery. I just want crispy lavaş, smoky fatty meats, sharp fresh salads and sunshine, please. Diyarbakır's city center is surrounded by ruins dating back further than ancient Rome. The walls were built by the Roman emperor Constantius II to keep opps out. Diyarbakır's name translates as "district of the Bakr people," an Arab tribe that conquered the city in the seventh century. Those same walls still stand in parts, although they're pretty beat up as tourists climb them to get a better look at the city. The view is beautiful, the greenery underneath stretches for quite some way; with mosque towers and apartment blocks spitted along the horizon, the connection between new and old. The park underneath is full of happy stray dogs lying on their backs catching the sun, and families having little picnics. There's definitely a rich history here: old brickwork and cobbled roads give it an ancient feel, the mosque slap bang in the middle of the "strip" is cool from heat-resistant brick. Men wash their hands, feet and faces under gold-spouted faucets, reciting Quran verses under their breath. It's a part of Türkiye that's deeply connected to Islam; women dress modestly, men in mosque attire. In a huge square near the mosque, men sit in groups drinking teas and flicking prayer beads.

I wander the streets on my first night just scoping the area, writing notes and figuring out tomorrow's moves. Diyarbakır is a city full of great food but there are the odd couple of scumbags. This is out in the sticks of Türkiye and, as much as I want to encourage you guys to enjoy these places first-hand, just be careful. Try to blend in and don't get caught slipping (like I did). I didn't get robbed, but I was moving like a bait tourist with my phone out, following a map at night while looking lost. I don't often feel vulnerable, nor do I get picked on—you've gotta be a little crazy to try and rob the 6ft 6 guy—but there were a couple of occasions where people tried it. Once, in broad daylight, walking along the main road, some guy put me in a headlock from behind, demanding all my money. He didn't hit me but, as we scuffled, he got his hand caught in the drawstring of my hoodie. As he pulled away, his hand pulled the drawstring taut. Well, at this point, I was fuming—and Kamil didn't raise no wuss. I threw (and landed) a very heavy left hand—and, well, he didn't get any money, but he might have got a sore chin. I obviously do not condone violence and like to think I'm the last person to get into a scrap. I'm usually good with using my words instead. In that situation though, I thought of what I'd tell Kamil if someone messed with his son. That might not make sense to some, but I grew up under a parent of a prisoner of war, who fought for his country when he didn't want to. In that respect, I can't let anyone ever screw me over. All I remember thinking is: if this guy is gonna shoot or stab me (which is a big thing in these parts of Türkiye), then I've got to leave him with a memory.

Every so often, I'm hit with the smell of rendering tail fat, spices and liver grilling hard and fast over charcoal. Men shout in the streets selling kapya biber seeds. After doing a little bit of research in the hotel room the night before, I found a must-try lahmacun spot called Lahmacun Merkezi, so I head there. I'm in the region of smoke, fat and bread so it seems only right that the first thing to eat here is lahmacun. I'm on the outskirts of where lahmacun was "invented." I say "invented" because all over this side of the world people have been smearing meat on to some form of bread for years. The lahmacun is crispy and the restaurant is boiling hot from the wood oven that's probably not been cold since the day they lit it. The youngest members of the family stretch the dough, Dad slaps on the meat with both hands, barely looking up to check his fire. Giving the lahmacun a final little reshape, he jolts them into the oven and picks out the last batch. He does this over and over again, for more than fourteen hours a day. It's served to me on a metal tray with intricate patterns engraved by hand, along with onions, parsley, a shaker full of pul biber and a cold steel mug of ayran. I garnish it, wrap it and eat it; the crunching noise loud in my

COSKUN
KUNDUR
LESILL
Tel: 293 63 7

head for about three minutes, chomping away. It's nothing like I've had at home—the base is paper thin, almost like a *carta di musica* (crispy cracker) in Italy. The meat is seasoned heavily and has little cubed chunks of tomato running through it, which prevents the meat mixture from becoming too wet. The lahmacun doesn't really roll like the ones at home do, more it cracks into shards, but has just enough moisture in the mix for it not to fall apart.

The door swings open every couple of minutes or so with hungry customers looking for a cheap meal. It's hot in here from the old wood oven and tight, tiled floor-to-ceiling dining room. I've seen the owner before on YouTube—and here he is; grinding away, glancing up to see another hungry customer walk through the door, eyes squinting from the intense heat, arms wet with sweat. The younger boys stretch out the dough for him, he pats down the meat, gives it one last touch before in it goes. It's the only wood-fired oven I've seen in Türkiye where the wood is elevated from the base—I guess that's to ensure that the thin crispy bottom doesn't burn and the meat is cooked off. He tells me his lahmacun is different because he uses two different types of flour, and his is the only lahmacun place here that washes the onions after cutting them for the salad. "I don't want you to be left with just the flavor of onion after the meal," he says with a caring head tilt and a serious look on his face.

There's a lot of İsot (Urfa biberi) in the lahmacun mixture. Being down the road from Urfa, and this being spice country, I'm really looking forward to eating something full of flavor and a bit on the spicy side. Not that Trabzon was bland, but I'm just used to punchy, bold flavors being at the forefront of a dish. This might be a bit premature, as I've only been here about three hours and eaten four lahmacun already, but when I die, forget heaven and send me to Diyarbakır.

MAKES 2

Pide come in loads of different shapes with loads of different toppings. This one is a breakfast variation, similar to one I ate on the outskirts of Istanbul in a local neighborhood pide spot called Lider Pide that specializes in making stuff on bread. The restaurant was full of locals, and being right next to a new development, there were loads of men in high-vis jackets devouring these.

If you've ever made a pizza, you're in luck, as this uses pretty much the same principles. The main thing about this pide is that it's served with a high-edged crust that's cut horizontally, so you pull the crust off and dip it into eggs to use as a spoon. I ate most of the dishes in this book in Türkiye on my own, and this was one that I wish I'd had someone with me to share the moment. Crispy crust, fresh runny eggs, a punch from sucuk, string pulls from the cheese and little pats of butter just allowed to rest over the top. Honestly, it's the best.

SUCUKLU YUMURTALI PIDE Breakfast pide

½ oz (15 g) fresh yeast, or ¼ oz (7 g) envelope active dry yeast
1½ cups (340 ml) lukewarm water
2 tbsp olive oil, plus extra for greasing
1 tsp sugar
4½ cups (550 g) all-purpose flour
coarse semolina, for shaping
sea salt

FOR THE FILLING
3¾ oz (110 g) cheese, for grating (Turks use kaşar peyniri, but mozzarella, Cheddar or any melty cheese will work)
4 eggs
1 sucuk (approx. 2¾ oz/ 80 g) Turkish breakfast sausage, pepperoni or any cured meat or chorizo, sliced
1 tbsp butter, plus extra melted for brushing

First, crumble the yeast into a bowl with the lukewarm water, olive oil and sugar and leave for 15 minutes to activate the yeast at room temperature.

In a separate bowl, sift in the flour and add a big pinch of sea salt. Make a well in the middle of the flour and slowly add the yeast mixture, stirring with a spoon or your hand, whatever you're more comfortable with. Once all the yeast mixture is in and the dough starts to form, tip it on to your work surface and knead until you have a soft, smooth dough. This will take about 15 minutes by hand, or mix in a stand mixer fitted with the dough hook for about 7 minutes. Transfer the dough to a large mixing bowl with a little oil in it so that the dough doesn't stick. Leave to proof at room temperature for 30 minutes, or until doubled in size.

Tip the dough out on to the work surface and split it into 2 equal pieces. Shape into balls, cover with a clean tea towel and allow to proof again, at room temperature, for 20 minutes until they're soft and full of air.

Scatter some semolina on your work surface and lay the dough on top. The key is establishing the crust first and then working away from it. About 1 inch (2.5 cm) in from the edge, push your fingers down deep all the way around the dough until you've made a clear crust shape, then flip the dough over and do the same on the other side (we do it on both sides to ensure that it will rise). Using the palms of your hands, put them into the crust line and pull the dough outwards in each direction, performing a quarter turn every time. The first time you do this it'll be a little weird looking in shape, but each time you turn the dough it'll ensure that the shape stays somewhat circular. Stretch the dough until the base is almost see-through. Repeat with the second dough ball.

I cooked my pides in a pizza oven at about 750°F (400°C), but if you're cooking in a regular oven, then preheat it to 425°F (220°C). Place the pides on a flat baking sheet. Bake for 4–6 minutes until slightly golden. The crusts will rise, and if the middle starts to rise up, too, don't worry about it. Remove from the oven, then add the fillings. Grate a layer of cheese on the bottom of each, crack 2 eggs on top of the cheese and season the eggs with sea salt. Return the pides to the oven for another 4 minutes to partially cook the eggs. Then add the sliced sucuk or cured meat, along with the butter and finish in the oven for another 4 minutes.

The oil from the sucuk should have bled and the sucuk curled, the egg whites set and a layer of melted butter formed on the top. Brush the crust of each pide with a little more butter. Cut the crust horizontally and serve.

SERVES 2

As excited as I was to be in Adana and eat Adana köfte where they originated, I'd also heard and seen loads about tost in Adana—full loaves of bread with spicy scrambled eggs, sucuk and Turkish ketchup, colored in a pan with loads of butter. It's the best way to start the day in Adana. There are loads of little stalls on the kerbside, not like a food market, more just scattered about the place. Where there is space, there's a chance to set up and earn a living.

You can use any bread you want for this recipe, but a good Turkish sandwich loaf called "somun" is the one you really want. Sucuk comes in many different shapes and sizes: sliced, whole or rings. I normally buy the sausages whole in links. If you can't find sucuk, then chorizo or merguez are the best replacements for fat and flavor. To make this recipe really authentic, try to get hold of all these ingredients and Turkish ketchup.

ADANA TOST Toasted Adana sandwich

- 1 loaf of somun ekmek, cut in half lengthways
- vegetable oil, for frying
- 4¼ oz (120 g) sucuk (Turkish breakfast sausage), cut into bite-sized pieces
- 1 beefsteak tomato, cut into bite-sized pieces
- 4 eggs
- 1 tbsp pul biber
- Turkish ketchup, to taste
- 1½ oz (40 g) kaşar peyniri or any other melty cheese, such as mozzarella, grated
- 3½ tbsp butter, softened
- sea salt

Set a frying pan over low heat and toast the bread halves slowly on both sides to give it a good color and crunch.

Stick a heavy-based frying pan over medium heat with very little oil, just a smidge to get the cooking process going. Sucuk is full of its own flavored fat and we want to keep this flavor running. Gently fry the sucuk until it's dark and the pan begins to fill with fat. Crank up the heat to high, add the tomato and a big pinch of salt and fry it hard and fast for about 45 seconds. We don't want to cook it all the way through and still want some texture. Crack in the eggs, then add the pul biber and season again with salt. Keep the heat high and stir-fry just until the eggs start to come together. We are going to toast the sandwich again after the base is cooked, so don't cook all the moisture out of the eggs.

Thinly spread the egg mixture on one side of the bread, then add a good squirt of ketchup and the grated cheese. Top with the other piece of bread and spread 2 tablespoons of the butter over the outside of the top half of the sandwich. Stick the sandwich back into the pan you toasted the bread in, buttered-side down. Put something heavy on top of the sandwich to weigh it down and keep it flat. Toast over medium heat for about 2 minutes until you can smell the butter starting to brown. Spread the remaining butter over the other side of the sandwich, then flip over the sandwich and cook for 2 minutes.

Lastly, spread some ketchup over the sandwich as you did with the butter and cook it on each side for 30 seconds. Keep the weight on top. The cooked ketchup and butter on the outside give the sandwich a sweetness and color. Cut in half down the middle to serve a generous breakfast sandwich for two.

MAKES 6

We've all had variations of a stuffed, savory bread. Gözleme is a half-moon-shaped, super-thin, and when done properly, crispy savory snack. It's pretty common in London now, having been accepted by the street food scene. Almost all over Türkiye, little aunties sit in shop windows on tiny stools making these over massive hot plates. Rolling out soft elastic dough and filling one side before folding and cooking, brushing with butter halfway through. If you ever buy one in a shop and they ask if you want it warm, make sure it's not being microwaved—the steam from the microwave makes them chewy and dense. Instead, take it home and reheat it in a dry pan.

Gözleme are delicious either as a quick grab-and-go snack, or a sit-down job with some fiery Turkish pickles. Here, I've given you my top three fillings—the ones I go to that never let me down.

GÖZLEME Filled flatbread

4 cups (500 g) all-purpose flour, plus extra for dusting
pinch of sea salt
1⅓ cups (320 ml) water
3 tbsp olive oil

EF VG V
FOR THE POTATO FILLING
2 lb 4 oz (1 kg) new potatoes: 1 lb 14 oz (850 g) peeled and chopped; 5½ oz (150 g) grated
olive oil, for frying
1 large white onion, finely diced
1½ tbsp pul biber
½ tbsp cumin seeds, toasted and crushed
½ tbsp superfine sugar
⅛ oz (5 g) flat-leaf parsley, chopped
sea salt

Sift the flour into a large mixing bowl, then mix in the salt. Make a well in the middle of the dry ingredients. Slowly add the water until the mixture comes together to form a dough.

Lightly dust a work surface with flour, then turn your dough out on to it. With floured hands, knead the dough for 10 minutes until it's uniform and smooth. Stick the dough to one side under a clean, dry tea towel. As there's no yeast in the dough, we're not looking for it to proof—just allowing it to rest.

For the potato filling
Stick the chopped potatoes in a pot and cover with salted water. Par-boil the potatoes until they are tender but still hold some resistance, testing with a knife. Strain the potatoes into a colander and allow them to steam.

Coat the base of a frying pan with olive oil. Over medium heat, get the oil to smoking point, then add the onion. Go in with a grind of salt and allow the onion to sweat until sweet and translucent. Once the onion is cooked, add the cooked potatoes to the frying pan. With the back of a spoon or a potato masher, gently crush them. Don't smash them completely—we want to increase their surface area but still have a chunky consistency.

Once the potatoes have come up to temperature, reduce the heat to low. We don't want to get color on our potatoes, instead we're trying to properly dry them out. Add the pul biber and cumin. Fry the spices for a couple minutes,

CONTINUES OVERLEAF

EF VG
FOR THE SPINACH FILLING
olive oil, for frying
1 large white onion, finely diced
2 bunches of large-leaf spinach
10½ oz (300 g) feta
zest of 1 lemon
1 tbsp pul biber
1 tsp freshly cracked black pepper
sea salt

EF
FOR THE MEAT FILLING
olive oil, for frying
14 oz (400 g) ground lamb
2 white onions, finely chopped
1 tbsp cumin seeds, toasted and crushed
2 tbsp pul biber
1 garlic clove, grated
1 large tomato, grated
1 tbsp sugar
¼ oz (10 g) parsley, chopped
sea salt

then add the grated potatoes and stir it through. To finish, stir in the sugar and parsley and remove from the heat. Check the seasoning—it should be spicy, sweet and salty with a little crunch from some remaining parts of raw potato.

For the spinach filling
In a little olive oil, sweat the onion in a frying pan over low-medium heat for 15–20 minutes until translucent. Add a grind of salt and ensure the onion doesn't catch any color.

Cut 1 inch (2.5 cm) off the ends of the spinach stalks and discard. Chop the spinach into ¾ inch (2 cm) pieces and then wash thoroughly with cold water to get rid of any grit. Make sure you dry the spinach; it's already got a high water content and any excess water on the spinach will dilute the filling.

Stick the dry spinach into a big mixing bowl. Crumble in the feta by rubbing it through your fingers. Add the lemon zest, pul biber and black pepper. Add the onion last—it doesn't really matter if it's still a bit warm. Get your hands into the mixture and be quite rough with it. Squeezing fistfuls of mixture together helps to break down the spinach and bring everything together.

For the meat filling
Warm a good glug of olive oil in a frying pan over high heat. Once the oil is smoking, add the ground lamb along with 2 big pinches of salt. The meat has different stages of cooking: the first part is about cooking off any excess moisture. You'll see that when the meat first starts to fry, it lets out a lot of liquid. We need to cook all that away to take us back to frying and getting color, which will build more flavor.

The second stage of cooking begins once the excess liquid has cooked off—you'll hear a change in the sizzle of a dry pan and notice that the meat is starting to color. Cook until you get an even, deep brown color on the meat. Remove the lamb from the pan and set aside in a bowl. Wipe down your pan with a sheet of paper towel, then stick in some more olive oil.

Over medium heat, sweat the onions in the oil for about 20 minutes to build a depth of sweetness.

Once the onions are cooked, return the lamb to the pan. Add the cumin and pul biber and fry gently for a couple of minutes until you notice they are fragrant and have infused the color of the oil. Add the garlic next and fry for about a minute, making sure it catches no color. Color will result in bitterness and it would be a shame, after all that time we've spent cooking the onions properly, to cover the flavor with burnt garlic.

The grated tomato goes in next and it won't need long to cook. Once all the tomatoey water has cooked off, we're good to finish with the sugar and parsley. Season to taste with salt and set aside to cool.

When you've finished making your chosen filling and the dough has been left to rest, you're ready to assemble. Split the dough into 6 dough balls. Put a generous handful of flour in a mound on a clean, dry work surface. Take one of the dough balls and roll it in the flour until it's fully covered.

Using a rolling pin, begin to roll out the dough ball, making sure it's coated in flour at all times to help it stretch. You've gotta be careful that it doesn't grow any bigger than the circumference of the frying pan you're going to cook it in. You'll want to use the biggest frying pan you've got—or if you've got a plancha, even better.

Roll out the dough until it's ⅟₁₆ inch (2 mm) thick. It doesn't have to be perfectly circular; the Turkish women who make these in shop windows are well-practiced in making 100+ gözleme a day for 20 years, so there's no way yours are going to look exactly the same.

I always work within one half of the pastry, gently dropping a spoonful of the filling in. Fold the dough over on itself like a calzone, leaving a ½ inch (1 cm) lip all the way around the side of the dough you're working on.

Using floured fingers, seal the sides of the dough together by pushing down the edges. If you want to make it look pretty, you can trim to neaten the edges, but it's not imperative. Repeat with the remaining dough balls and filling.

Heat your biggest dry frying pan (or plancha) over a medium heat—you don't want it smoking hot though, as this will burn any excess flour. Pick up a gözleme and give it a couple of taps to dust off any excess flour.

Stick the gözleme in the pan and cook over medium heat for 2–3 minutes on each side until crispy. You're looking for a nice leopard print coverage in areas that catch and turn golden. Once both sides are crispy, use a pastry brush to coat the outside with a little olive oil. I like the inconsistency in gözleme's texture; some bits are soft and chewy and others are super-crunchy. Repeat to cook the remaining gözleme.

I like to serve gözleme with tangy pickles (see pages 28-29 for homemade), which you can easily pick up in any Turkish supermarket if you don't have homemade ones.

MAKES 12

No, it's not a Turkish pizza—there's no cheese.

Back in the days when these were 99p ($1.50) each in my local kebap shop, I used to have lahmacun nights with my family or the boys. For years I didn't bother trying to make them, but once I realized how easy they were to make, I've rarely bought them since. It's a good little recipe for a party, this one. You can do all the base work in advance for guests to choose their own toppings.

Lahmacun are served all over Türkiye, but mostly in southeastern Anatolia. Some varieties are small—about the size of a CD—some are huge and oblong. The toppings vary, but lahmacun are often served with mint or pistachios to finish. For me, this is just a really good, standard lahmacun recipe: spicy meat, sweet vegetables and a soft but crispy bottom.

LAHMACUN Meat flatbread

- 8 cups (1 kg) all-purpose flour, plus extra for dusting
- big pinch of sea salt
- 2⅓ cups (560 ml) lukewarm water
- ¼ oz (7 g) fresh yeast, or 1 tsp (3.5 g) active dry yeast
- 1 tbsp sugar
- 2 tbsp olive oil, plus extra for greasing

Take all the vegetables, the tomato, garlic and parsley for the topping and stick them in a food processor. I don't bother taking the seeds out of the peppers for this one—let 'em stay, they won't harm anyone. Blend together and transfer to a mixing bowl.

To the same mixing bowl, add the ground lamb and spices, along with the pepper and 2 big pinches of salt. Mix the blended vegetables and lamb together for a couple of minutes until it's uniform in color. The mixture gets better the longer it sits in the fridge, so you can do this a day in advance if you have time to.

To make the dough, sift the flour into a large mixing bowl, making sure there are no lumps. Add the big pinch of salt and mix.

In a separate bowl, mix together the lukewarm water, crumbled yeast, sugar, a big pinch of salt and the olive oil. Leave to sit for 10 minutes for the yeast to activate.

Add the yeast mixture into the dry mixture, little by little, adding more of the liquid when the flour mixture gets stiff. Once all the liquid has been added, knead the dough in the bowl—picking up any bits of flour around the sides or stuck to the bottom.

FOR THE TOPPING

2 Corno di Toro red peppers, chopped
2 Charleston light green salad peppers, chopped
4 sivri biber (green peppers), chopped
2 white onions, chopped
1 large bull's heart tomato, chopped
4 garlic cloves
1 bunch of flat-leaf parsley, chopped
1 lb 7 oz (650 g) ground lamb
1 tbsp pul biber
1 tbsp kırmızı toz biber (Turkish paprika)
1 tbsp cumin seeds, toasted and crushed
1 tsp freshly cracked black pepper
sea salt

TO GARNISH

½ bunch of parsley, chopped
2 white onions, thinly sliced
juice of ½ lemon
sprinkle of chile flakes

Tip the dough out on to a clean, floured work surface and knead for 10 minutes—pulling and folding the dough back on itself. Transfer the dough to a bowl and cover with a clean, dry tea towel. Allow the dough to proof in a warm, dark place for 40 minutes until doubled in size.

Once the dough has risen, turn it out on to a clean, floured work surface. Roll the dough into a long sausage shape, about the same thickness as a sausage roll, then portion into twelve 3½ oz (100 g) portions. Don't bother weighing each one: weigh the first one and use that as a guide to measure the rest by eye.

Roll the portioned dough into little balls. Stick them on a lightly oiled pan and cover with a damp tea towel. Allow the balls to proof for 15 minutes until they're soft, light and fluffy.

Preheat the oven to 475°F (240°C), ensuring it's properly hot before you start the next step.

Making sure there is flour on your work surface and rolling pin, roll a ball of dough out into a thin pizza shape, about 1⁄16 inch (2 mm) thick. Take a big handful of the meat topping and spread it thinly across the base of the dough, starting from the middle and working out towards the edges. It's key that your oven is hot by this point, as we don't want the meat mixture to sit on the dough for too long, making it soggy. Lahmacuns cook quickly and we want a nice crispy bottom.

You can cook the lahmacun on either a dry baking sheet or a pizza stone. However you decide to do it, just make sure the pan has been sitting in the preheated oven until it is hot before you place the lahmacun on top. Cook the lahmacun for 4–6 minutes until the meat mixture is cooked and you've got a nice crispy base on the dough. Repeat the process for the remaining dough balls and meat topping.

I like to garnish lahmacuns with some chopped parsley, thinly sliced onions, a big drizzle of lemon juice and a sprinkle of chile flakes.

EF V

MAKES 12

My nan used to make these in Cyprus. Plain ones, like in this recipe, are usually served with breakfast. For dessert in Cyprus, sometimes these are served with a sweetened tahini on the inside. They're almost like a Turkish roti. They are super-easy to make and go well with everything.

KATMER Layered butter flatbread

4½ cups (550 g) bread flour, plus extra for dusting
1½ cups (350 ml) water
1 tsp baking powder
3 tbsp butter, melted
3 tbsp oil, plus extra for greasing
sea salt

Sift the flour into a mixing bowl. Mix the water and baking powder together. Season the flour with a big pinch of salt, then pour in the water and bring the dough together with a spoon. It's quite a wet dough, so continue to mix it in the bowl until it comes together. Cover the dough in the bowl with a clean tea towel and let it rest at room temperature for 10 minutes.

Tip the dough out on to a floured work surface and knead for 5 minutes just until the dough starts to smooth out. Roll the dough into a large sausage shape, the approximate length of a baguette, and cut the dough into 4 equal pieces. Cut each of those pieces into 3, so you have 12 pieces in total. Shape the little dough bits into balls and let them rest at room temperature, on an oiled tray covered with a tea towel, for another 10 minutes.

Roll each dough ball out into large thin pizza shapes, about 8 inches (20 cm) in length. Using the tip of your knife, make little horizontal slashes in the dough about ½ inch (1 cm) long, quite close together and all over, like a rainwater pattern on a window.

Mix the melted butter and oil together and brush some over the dough. Turn the dough 90 degrees so the slashes are now horizontal. Roll the dough like a tight burrito so you're left with a sausage shape. Working from one side to the other, spiral the dough in on itself like the shell of a snail and give it a good press down. Repeat this process with all the dough pieces and let them rest for another 30 minutes. Cover the dough in plastic wrap while resting. If you want to make these in advance, you can pop them in the fridge.

On a lightly floured work surface, roll out the dough spirals into circles the size of a CD.

Heat a dry frying pan over medium heat. Once the frying pan is up to temperature, add a flatbread and cook, flipping every 1–2 minutes, until brown and crispy. This will take about four turns in total, making sure to keep the heat on medium as the butter will burn otherwise. Once cooked, put it in a clean tea towel to help it steam while you cook the remaining flatbreads, then add them to the tea towel. Serve warm.

MAKES 8

We all love flatbreads. They're easy to make and go a long way. I wouldn't go as far as comparing these breads to brioche, but the milk makes them rich and comforting. Great for a sandwich, a BBQ or just for dipping. Just really soft, milk-enriched, doughy beautiful bread.

SÜTLÜ EKMEK Milk flatbreads

4 cups (500 g) all-purpose flour, plus extra for dusting
⅔ cup (160 ml) milk
½ oz (15 g) fresh yeast, or ¼ oz (7 g) envelope active dry yeast
heaped 2 tsp sugar
⅔ cup (160 ml) cold water
1 tbsp olive oil, plus extra for greasing
sea salt

Sift the flour into a mixing bowl and season with a pinch of salt.

Warm the milk gently in a pan; don't boil it, it only really needs to come up to body temperature.

In a bowl, combine the crumbled yeast, the sugar, cold water and olive oil and stir together. Leave to sit for 15 minutes for the yeast to do its thing and react with the sugar. Add the room-temperature milk and give it a good mix.

Make a well in the flour, pour in the yeast mixture and bring the dough together using a wooden spoon. Once the dough has come together and the bowl is clean, tip the dough out on to a work surface.

Throw a little bit of flour over the work surface and knead the dough for at least 15 minutes until it's nice and smooth. Transfer the dough to a bowl with a little olive oil to stop it from sticking and cover with plastic wrap. Leave the dough to proof somewhere warm for about 40 minutes, or until doubled in size.

Knock back the dough and shape it into a 12 inch (30 cm) long sausage, then portion the dough into 8 evenish dough balls. Cover with a clean, wet tea towel and leave to proof for another 30 minutes.

I like these flatbreads thick and doughy, so roll out the dough balls to about ⅛ inch (3 mm) thick. The thicker they are, the doughier they will be and the thinner they are, the crispier they will be.

Cook a flatbread in a dry frying pan over medium heat for 2–3 minutes on one side; the first side is about building color. Then flip the flatbread, which will puff up and then sink. Once it's done that, it's good to go. Wrap it in some clean paper towels to keep warm while you cook the remaining flatbreads. Serve warm.

laGERMANIA

V

MAKES 2 PIDES

You know that bread you always see in Turkish grocery stores, the one that's oval-shaped, with a diamond pattern and sesame seeds on top? Well, that's this. Although the name is a nod to the holy month, Ramazan pidesi is available all year round and most Turks buy it from the bakery. During the month of Ramadan, it's made at home and is usually the first thing people break their fast with. I know making bread can feel intimidating, but this is a very easy recipe. The hardest part is the shaping but, even if you don't get the diamond pattern right, I promise you this is a versatile recipe that you'll use again and again.

RAMAZAN PIDESI Ramadan bread

- 5¾ cups (700 g) Turkish flour or bread flour, plus extra for dusting
- 2 grinds of sea salt
- 1 cup (240 ml) warm water
- ¾ cup (180 ml) warm milk
- ¼ oz (10 g) fresh yeast, or 1½ tsp (5 g) active dry yeast
- 1 tbsp sugar
- 1 tbsp olive oil
- 1 egg yolk, beaten
- 4 tsp mixed white and black sesame seeds

Sift the flour into a large mixing bowl. Add the salt and give it a whisk to distribute. In a separate bowl, mix together the warm water, milk, crumbled yeast, sugar and olive oil. Set aside for 30 minutes for the yeast to activate.

Make a well in the middle of the flour, then slowly pour the yeast mixture into the flour. Using your hands, bring the dough together until the sides and the bottom of the bowl are clean and no streaks of flour remain.

Tip the dough out on to a lightly floured work surface. Knead the dough for about 5 minutes until smooth. Round the dough into a ball, then transfer to a bowl. Cover with a clean, dry tea towel and leave to proof in a warm, dark place for 30 minutes until doubled in size.

When the dough has risen, you'll see that it is pillowy and full of air. We need to punch out the first round of air and proof again to let the flavors build and start the shaping process. To do this, tip the dough out on to a floured work surface and cut the dough into 2 equal pieces.

Dust 2 roasting pans with a sprinkling of flour, before placing a dough ball in the middle of each. Lay a clean, dry tea towel over the top of each pan and leave the dough to proof in a warm, dark place for a further 45 minutes until doubled in size.

Preheat the oven to 425°F (220°C).

When the dough balls have finished their second proof, it's time to start forming the shape. Using floured hands, push downwards into each dough ball to make indentations for the crust, leaving a 1¼ inch (3 cm) gap between the edge and the middle.

Once you've formed the crust, it's time to stretch out each dough ball. Using the crust as a handle, pull the sides out, alternating between vertical and horizontal pulls, to make a large, oval shape about 16 inches (40 cm) in length.

Using your fingers, make indentations across the center in straight lines, about 2 inches (5 cm) apart, creating a diamond pattern.

Generously brush the breads with beaten egg yolk, all the way to the outer side of the crusts. Sprinkle over the sesame seeds and bake the breads for 20 minutes; one on the middle rack and one on the bottom. The middle loaf will darken quicker, so it's important to swap their positioning after 10 minutes of baking.

To check each bread is cooked, turn over and give it a little tap. If it sounds hollow, it's ready. If not, return to the oven for a further 5 minutes. When the bread is cooked, remove it from the oven and leave to cool on a wire rack before slicing. Bread is always best consumed on the day it was baked, but wrap whatever you're left with in plastic wrap. If the bread gets stale, I use it to make toast or croutons.

FİYATLARIMIZA
KATMA DEĞER VERGİSİ
DAHİLDİR
ÖZEL USULSÜZLÜK
CEZASI LEVHASI
ALSANCAK İLKOKULU
DIBAL

06

MEAT

URFA (Southeastern Türkiye)

For the next part of my trip, I've decided to get around by jumping on buses. It's the cheapest way around Türkiye, costing about $10 in total, no matter the duration. Although Türkiye has bullet trains, the journeys don't really make sense as they don't stop in smaller destinations or towns, especially on the side of the country that I'm on; taking you to only either Ankara or Istanbul. The buses are comfortable, with rows of double seats and singles. Men can't sit next to women unless they're traveling together, which I think is a nice touch. Everyone should be able to get on public transportation and know they're safe.

I jump on a three-and-a-bit hour bus journey to Sanliurfa. The weather's getting hotter as we're driving through the mountains, the reflection of the sun bouncing off windscreens on the oncoming lanes. I spend a lot of the journey playing Nintendo and looking out the window. I don't play my Nintendo at home at all, but when I'm traveling it's an essential. I'm excited for Urfa: its spicy food and the celebration of kapya peppers. İsot (or Urfa biberi), is made the same way as pul biber. Peppers are left to dry in the sun, deseeded and then crushed. Urfa biberi is made exactly the same way—but once crushed, is left in the sun to dry out again until turning black and fiery. It has a distinctive flavor with chocolate notes, a hum of heat and an earthy vibe. It's used in pretty much everything in Urfa.

My first impression of Urfa is that the people are friendly and accommodating; I've already had multiple invites back to the village to "come make Çiğ köfte with my mom." It's a hot city full of history, tail fat smoke and seasoned bread—my first stop in kebap country on this food pilgrimage. Men wear a classic mustache here, in the style of İbrahim Tatlıses, the imperator. Tatlıses or, as he's often called, İbo, is the straight Elton John of Türkiye. He's a Turkish singer, actor and TV host; triple threat. İbo was born in Urfa to an Arab father and a Kurdish mom, and bridged the gap between three different cultures, incorporating an Arabesque style in mainstream Turkish folk music, often singing in Kurdish, too. Although I described him as a straight Elton John—don't get it twisted: he's a gangster. With a failed assassination attempt leaving him with only half of his mobility, he's still out there performing and bringing back *The İbo Show* after a long hiatus. İbo's music played a big part in my childhood; it's celebrated by Turks in most Turkish households at weddings and parties. He's a living legend of Turkish culture and seems cool, to be fair. Not only is there a big Kurdish community in Urfa, but also Arab. As well as food being spicy, it's meat heavy and there's not a loaf of bread in sight. Bread here is purely used to dip or scoop. This is lavaş country, baby.

I have a lot of trouble understanding my first cab driver here, as the k's in the alphabet have turned to throaty g's. I arrive in Urfa early so dump my bags, check out the indoor pool and head out to find a kebap shop. I've already got a few funny looks here, probably because I'm still wearing shorts and the Turks consider this pretty cold winter weather. I get the occasional "Oh, ha!," which I guess is the same as a "Jeez!". Turks are generally quite blunt. If you look fat, they'll tell you.

"*Selamünaleyküm*," I say in a deep voice as I duck and shimmy my body through the doorway of a kebap shop that I find near the closed market. I feel like a supermodel—'cause all the guys in this kebap shop turn to look at me, eyes glazed, mouths a little open. "*Aleyküm selâm*." "Just me, *abi*." The young waiter, who's probably about eighteen, takes me around the corner to sit in a little wooden booth. "I'll have the terbiyesiz tavuk, haşhaş kebapı and a patlıcan kebabı." 'That's a lot of food, man—are you sure?," he asks with an upward hand gesture that says, "You're the boss." He hears from my accent that I'm not from around here. "Germany? Holland? Saudi?" I explain I'm Cypriot and from London. "You speak great Turkish." I think my Turkish is pretty shit, but I'll take it. I hear him recite my order to the boys at the mangal and there's a few snickers. He comes back with a roughly chopped salad and a glass of ayran before plonking a huge bottle of water on the table.

We get talking and I tell him I'm a chef, which excites him. He gets out his phone and gives me a follow on Insta.

My food comes out on a cheap steel dish with a high base. It's basically an elevated kebap. I might have overshot my order, but it smells fucking great. The terbiyesiz chicken is dark and crispy, almost like Japanese *yakatori,* which comes from the soy sauce. The haşhaş kebabı is steaming hot and barely holding together. Then there's the celebrated patlıcan kebabı—huge chunks of dark, shriveled and soft eggplant, with little balls of köfte in between. Fire-roasted red chiles, quartered onions, a bunch of parsley, all sit on paper-thin fresh lavaş. I smile, looking at the mountain of food, and the waiter and I share a little laugh.

I'm genuinely excited, like opening an Xbox on Christmas Day. I live for this shit. There aren't many things that bring me joy the way this food does: steaming meats, tightly-wet flatbread and

an eat-it-the-way-you-want garnish. I've never eaten something as simple and satisfying as this eggplant kebap. I peel the shriveled skin from the eggplant, scrape out its flesh, stick it in a piece of lavaş, before crumbling in some meat. I add salt, onions, parsley, fire-roasted chiles before wrapping it and sticking it in my mouth. The terbiyesiz kebap is fucking confusing—salty, soft, spicy and very Japanese-tasting—but it is one of those dishes I'll never forget. Before coming to Urfa, I had only tried poor imitations of this particular type of kebap. I wrap it in lavaş with chiles and parsley, biting big bits of onion in between mouthfuls. Sensational. It's crude food of pure necessity: a couple of vegetables cooked over a fire served with humble bread—which reminds me of home. It's comforting for me, as this food has flavors that have been consistent throughout my life, either in north London or north Cyprus.

Urfa's food is full of good fat that enhances the flavor as it cooks. The köfte are crumbly and smoky—but retain a sort of plainness, in a good way—it's just about the right amount of fat to good-quality meat. Success in simplicity: only a few ingredient decisions, but important ones. It's similar to doing a hamburger well: you've gotta think about buns—brioche, sesame or demi? Crappy cheese or fancy cheese? Cooked onion or raw? Realistically, none of that actually matters if the meat isn't right, and it all comes down to the ratio being the right amount of fat to cheap cut. If the chew is missing, the burger won't caramelize. It's *that* level of attention to detail, starting at the very humble roots. There's confidence in this cooking: the intentional chopping of the meat, the precise ratios, the light seasoning. I believe that, at a kebap shop, the most important things are the meat suppliers, using seasonal vegetables, and fresh bread. Those things are non-negotiables—the fundamentals that make your food better than everyone else's. And this place has it.

That being said, it's pretty hard for my kebap comparisons to hold up internationally—the quality of the meat in Türkiye stands out due to the local suppliers and the diet of the animals, directly influencing the flavor. I think the problem with most kebap shops back home (minus a few—honorable mention to my guys at Mangal and the cousins in Best Kebap, Stoke Newington) is that Turks only trust Turks. Need a mechanic? I've got a Turk that'll do it cheaper. Dentist? I'm defo going to a Turk. Even doctors—we'll go to a Turk. There's a tiny bit of ignorance behind it—Turks know best, etc.—but, if you're from a mixed background, I think you'll know what I mean. Ultimately, it comes down to ingrained trust issues, but they stem from looking after each other and being in the same situation, fresh off the boat. Of course, you're gonna seek out people of shared heritage, who you trust aren't gonna fuck you over. However, as sweet as that is, I think it restricts kebap shops from branching out and meeting great meat suppliers outside of their immediate community. Everything is from so and so's buddy whose cousin used to be a delivery driver working for a wholesaler—he doesn't sell the best quality meat, but he's Turkish. I've got dreams of opening a döner kebap shop and, if I sell enough copies of this book, I'm gonna fucking do it. I don't want it to be pretentious, and I don't want to put my spin on something that's been around for centuries. I want to do it in a way that works for everyone; traditional but in a different setting using little tricks of the trade: ex-dairy meat, aged fats, seasonal tomatoes, bread that's made in-house. There'll be no seats, and everything will be served on paper. Just me and a couple of handsome gents slinging homemade döner and laughing all the way to the motherfucking bank (not in an evil, villainous way—more in an everyone-wins-ethically kinda way).

It turns out that the waiter at the restaurant, is the son of the shop's owner. He explains to his dad that I'm a chef from London before he comes and sits at my table. Unwrapping a kebap of his own, packed with parsley, he shows me all the stuff he's done on YouTube and TV—appearances where he's talked about opening a new restaurant. We sit for a couple of hours talking life, and he invites me back in the morning for a liver breakfast. Liver is a huge thing in these parts of Türkiye but, unfortunately, it's not a Hasan thing. I make sure to stop by on the day I leave Urfa to say thank you like a true gentleman, tipping mad heavy.

SERVES 4

TERBIYESIZ TAVUK Rude chicken

I didn't really know what to expect when traveling in Türkiye; I went to cities knowing little about the food and the specialties. I was told about this dish by two locals in the sauna at my hotel. I was swimming away, with my little swimming cap on (although I'm not very streamlined, I'm actually a good swimmer) and these two guys were trying to swim and stopped me and asked if I could give them a couple of tips. (Told you I was a good swimmer.) Anyway, we got chatting and our conversation carried us to the sauna. They told me all the things I should do in Urfa and they mentioned terbiyesiz tavuk (rude chicken). I laughed wondering how rude a chicken could be. They told me it's to do with the unconventional way it's marinated in milk for tenderness, then soy sauce to season. I said my goodbyes and off I went the next day on the hunt for some rude chicken. I ate in a kebap shop in the fruit and veg market, filled with men and women after a hard day's work selling and moving goods. The chicken was super-soft, subtly salty from soy and with a little hum from the Urfa chile flakes. A kebap I won't forget. So, here's my take on it.

I made this recipe with a mixture of thighs and drumsticks, which I bought whole from the butcher and skinned and boned myself, but if you ask nicely your butcher will sort that out for you. Now, obviously we all have to live within our means but I'll always buy free-range chicken, whether that's the supermarket brand in fancier packaging or from a butcher. The meat's more flavorful, the texture is different and I know this would make an environmental health officer's skin crawl, but it means you can ever-so-slightly undercook your chicken and get away with it. I ate a lot of soft, bouncy, pinkish meat in Türkiye and survived to tell the tale.

I also feel like free-range chicken cooks better under intense heat, and another thing I learned in Türkiye is that the method Kamil taught me how to cook meat is non-existent there. They keep it instinctive. Is it raging hot? Is the meat on sticks? Then what are you waiting for? The mangal men in Türkiye are the equivalent of the sushi masters of Japan. Years of the craft, honing their expertise, the little pieces of attention to detail that aren't noticed by the untrained eye. Knowing when to turn skewers, the visual cues when the meat is cooked, when to season, the subtle changes of smell from the smoke, the color of the smoke when fat's rendering or cooking too quickly. This isn't two American men drinking canned beer, talking American football, covering meats in mustard and dry rubs, loading slow cooks into electric smokers with meat sensors before the game starts. These guys sit in front of fierce fires all day, forearms hot to the touch and faces creased from squinting in front of the heat.

CONTINUES OVERLEAF

I'm actually desperate to be one of those guys. If I were to die tomorrow, I feel like one of my biggest regrets would be not backing myself enough to open a little takeout kebap place. Not a new-school modern one with a blue suede interior and gold finishes, which seems to be the thing in North London at the moment. Just a no-frills, food-does-the-talking type spot. I like the way my dad, Turks and many other nationalities just make shit happen. In Urfa, a huge BBQ setup hums with ventilation fans, sucking out air and pumping it onto the street. The mangal man sits in a well-worn office chair (not ideal, but practical) on top of cardboard box flooring which lines the area to make cleanup easier. There are twelve shitty booths across the front of the mangal, a couple of mismatching tables in the corner and the food wrapped in branded wax paper. For me, that's the dream. Although I've come on a hunt scouting new recipes for this book, I find myself chasing the smell of newly burning charcoal and listening for knives pit-patting, making salads on the wrong-color chopping boards. I'm coming home with a good number of recipe ideas, but an even bigger chip on my shoulder.

- 1 lb 2 oz (500 g) skinless, boneless chicken thighs and/or drumsticks
- 1 cup (220 ml) milk
- 4 tbsp soy sauce
- 2 tbsp İsot (Urfa biberi) or pul biber
- 2 garlic cloves
- 1 banana shallot
- sunflower or vegetable oil, for drizzling
- sea salt

TO SERVE

- lavaş or pita bread
- fire-roasted red and green chiles

Cube the chicken into bite-sized pieces, making sure there are no bits of bone if you're using drumsticks and no cartilage if you're using thighs. Add the chicken to a bowl with the milk, soy sauce and chile flakes. Grate in the garlic and shallot. Now, I beg you, please just marinate this in the fridge for at least 24 hours and see the difference it makes. I know you've not got anything to compare it to right now, but trust me, I did the hard work for you. The milk will break down the chicken a little and make it super-soft, and the soy will almost brine the chicken.

Skewer up the chicken, pinching the meat as your skewer, making sure the meat doesn't move when you spin the skewers. Drizzle over some sunflower or vegetable oil and season lightly with salt, remember the soy will already be salty so don't go heavy with it. Light a BBQ and as soon as the charcoal reaches a 5 count (see page 246), spread the charcoal evenly. Stick the skewers on, turning them every minute or so. I really like the way the soy caramelizes under the heat of the BBQ, giving little bitter dark tones. The chicken will take about 6–8 minutes. Make sure you keep turning it and don't build color too quickly. Burnt edges are fine near the end of the cook, but not at the beginning.

Let the skewers rest for a minute or so on some warm bread—lavaş or pita—once they come off the BBQ. I served mine with the meat juice, bread and some fire-roasted red and green chiles.

SERVES 4

Köftes in Turkish households are super common and enjoyed up to three times a week. They're served all over the country, with little changes in fat-to-meat ratios or seasonings. Affordable, easy, served with whatever you please. This recipe is my at-home köftes—easy prep, easy cook, double satisfied. Stick 'em in bread with some muhammara (see page 41), eat them over rice or just with a plate of raw onions and a couple of fire-roasted chiles.

Please don't buy ground cumin—it's old, stale and lifeless. Buy the seeds, as they last longer, and toast them when you want them. Please do that for this recipe and any other recipe I tell you to put cumin in. Thanks.

KÖFTE Turkish meatballs

- 1 lb 10 oz (750 g) lamb shoulder, fat on, ground (ask your butcher to do this for you)
- 1 tbsp sea salt
- 2 tbsp pul biber
- 1 tbsp cumin seeds, toasted and crushed
- 13 oz (380 g) white onions
- 6 garlic cloves

Put your ground lamb in a bowl and add all the dry ingredients. Grate the onions on the biggest side of a box grater. Stick the grated onion in a clean kitchen cloth or tea towel and squeeze out all the excess liquid (any liquid will stop our köftes emulsifying), meaning we'll get beautiful bouncy balls of spiced meat. Add the onion to the lamb mixture. Microplane the garlic in, too. The reason we are grating the onions and garlic is that we want the flavors to evenly spread through the mixture, no chunks here and there, so every köfte is uniform.

Mix the köftes by hand if you can, for 15 minutes. The heat from your hands will help combine the mixture. Be quite aggressive with the mixture, squelch it through your hands, fold it back on itself. I like to do this to music. Three or four songs in and you're good, however, if you're like me and you need visual cues, the lamb fat in the meat will have distributed enough for the mixture to look like a mystery meat frozen burger. The köftes are good to go from that point, but for best results I like to let mine marinate in the fridge overnight.

Shaping the köftes is entirely up to you. Köftes come in all different shapes and sizes across Türkiye, but when I'm banging them out for a family meal, I normally go with little UFO burger shapes. It's easier to shape the köftes with wet hands, so make sure you've got a little bowl of water knocking about to dip your hands in once in a while. I'd normally go for 3–4 köftes per person, weighing 2¼–3¼ oz (60–90 g) each.

You can pan-fry or bake, but for best results defo cook these over charcoal. A 3 count will do here (see page 246), as you don't want to make them too crispy on the outside too early. Let them slowly cook, creating loads of smoke from the fat dropping into the fire. Keep them moving, turning every 30 seconds or so. Once the köftes are a nice brown and have a little firm tension to the touch, they are ready. Patience is key with building flavor and Turkish BBQs.

MAKES ABOUT 50 KÖFTES/SERVES 4–6

On the outskirts of Trabzon, there's a small town called Akçaabat famous for its köfte, so obviously I had to go check it out. It was a 20-minute drive from my hotel, and to be fair, there wasn't much to see or do in Trabzon besides eating cheese or fried fish and seeing mountains. The köfte are cooked over a dying heat, slow and steady with not much color but taking on loads of smoke. The köftes themselves are soft and juicy, packed with punchy garlic and onion. In Türkiye, köftes are normally served with muhammara (see page 41), bread and a plate of thinly sliced white onions. If I were to choose a salad out of the book to go with the köftes, I'd go for the Piyaz on page 48.

Kindly ask your butcher to debone the ribs for you but to keep the fat on—it's important that the ground meat has gone through the grinder at least twice. This will help the mixture emulsify when we mix it. If the butcher is willing to do all of this for you, get them to grind the fat with the meat, too, so it's all evenly spread and uniform. You can buy the breadcrumbs but, living in a Turkish household, there's always some sort of stale bread on the windowsill. Blend the stale bread into breadcrumbs and it's good to go.

AKÇAABAT KÖFTESI Köfte from Akçaabat

- 1 lb 9 oz (700 g) beef ribs, ground (ask your butcher to do this for you, see intro)
- 2 lb 4 oz (1 kg) lamb ribs, ground (ask your butcher to do this for you, see intro)
- 10½ oz (300 g) lamb tail fat, or anything the butcher is willing to give away
- 10 garlic cloves
- 2 large onions, grated and drained
- ⅔ cup (80 g) dried breadcrumbs (see intro)
- ¾ tsp baking soda
- oil, for brushing
- sea salt and pepper

When you get home with your bag of ground meat mixed with the fat, grate in the garlic, then add the drained onions and breadcrumbs. Season the mixture heavily and give it a good mix. Knead it, slap it about or, my favorite, stick it in the pan and give it the monkey knuckle using all your bodyweight and force from your shoulders. Just imagine you're a gorilla walking or something. When I say a good mix, I mean like 15 minutes. We're helping the mixture to become one uniform piece of meat, meaning that it's consistent and pieces won't break away when it comes to cooking the köfte over the fire. The mixture will stick to whatever you're mixing it in, and after about 15 minutes it will all come together and hold its shape. Finally, stick in the baking soda and mix that in, too. The baking soda helps the köfte to remain juicy and softens the meat. For best results, marinate the mixture in the fridge overnight.

The following day, shape the köftes. I do little sausages but you can serve them in little meatball shapes, if you like. For the sausages, weigh out 1¾ oz (50 g) of köfte mixture, then shape it your hands to make sure the mixture has come together and there's no air bubbles. Round by rolling on a chopping board. This mixture makes about 50 köftes.

Oil and season the köftes, then grill them nice and slow on a BBQ over a 4 count (see page 246), turning every minute or so. These köftes will produce loads of smoke, which will flavor them as it fucks off into the air, burning a hole in the ozone. The köftes will need to grill for at least 8–10 minutes. They should be dark and a little crispy, with clear juices. Enjoy.

EF GF

SERVES 4

This was one of the best things I ate on my travels, sat in a huge restaurant surrounded by hand-painted ceilings, trays of baklava and polished dark wooden furniture. I sat at a communal table with winter sun beaming in. The waiter brought this over and it glistened in the sun, still sizzling, smells of tail fat and desperate for bread. Really simple but right up my street. In Türkiye, the onions are small, sweet onions, which aren't that easy to find in the UK unless you go to organic shops. Instead, I've used shallots, which carry more sugar and their tough skins make them ideal for cooking over fire.

SOĞAN KEBABI Onion kebap

- 14 oz (400 g) banana shallots, unpeeled
- 3 tbsp İsot (Urfa biberi)
- 1 tbsp sea salt
- drizzle of pomegranate molasses
- kebap meat mixture (see page 176)

Preheat the oven to 350°F (180°C).

Stick the shallots in a roasting pan and put them in the oven for about 25 minutes. We want the shallots to cook slowly to prevent them popping open and keep all the sweetness on the inside. Once the shallots are cooked, allow them to cool fully before using. I find it works best if you give the shallots some time in the fridge, probably about 4 hours. I left mine overnight, along with the meat mixture, just for the flavors to develop.

Once the shallots are chilled, peel and split them down the middle leaving the root intact. Spread the shallots open and season the insides with salt, a drizzle of olive oil and a tiny touch of pomegranate molasses. They don't need loads as they have sugar in them already, just enough for them to go dark and sticky. Skewer the shallots straight through the root, making sure they hold. The idea is that you should be able to turn them with no dangly bits.

Skewer the meat in the same way we do for the kebap recipe on page 176.

Set up a BBQ to a 2 count (see page 246). Stick the shallots on first as they'll need a little longer to cook. I start skin-side down because the skin can take the heat and let the shallots come up to temperature. Flip them every 2 minutes or so until the shallots start to go a lovely caramel color but are still soft. We're not looking for crispy shallots here but ones that are soft, sweet and warm.

Cook the meat according to the instructions on page 176.

Plate up the meat and the shallots on the same plate, I like to leave a little piece of lavaş bread on the bottom just to suck up all those juices.

Peel a shallot, break a köfte, wrap it up and dip it in the resting juices on the bottom of the plate.

MAKES 10 BÖREKS

We grew up eating Turkish pastries from Turkish food centers and at auntie's birthdays where there would always be a plate of homemade (or bought-in) assortments. I don't often do pastry stuff, mostly because my oven at home doesn't have a fan and it's just pretty hard to get anything like a börek to cook properly. I love böreks; they're delious, full of butter and a seasoned meat or veg mix. Great for all times of day or even as a gift to a neighbor.

BÖREK Mixed meat pastries

- olive oil, for frying
- 2 lb 10 oz (1.2 kg) ground lamb
- 1 lb 2 oz (500 g) finely diced red onions
- 2 tbsp pul biber
- 1 tbsp dried flowering oregano
- 1 tsp sugar
- 10 sheets of filo pastry (see page 23 for homemade)
- 1 egg, beaten
- sea salt and pepper

Set a large frying pan over high heat and add a good glug of olive oil. Stick in the ground lamb and fry for 20 minutes until it's released all its liquid and begins to fry again. Cook out all the moisture and take it back to frying to make it dark and crispy. When the lamb is crispy and starting to pop like popcorn, season heavily with salt and pepper. Set aside.

I really hate adding vegetables into already-cooked meat and expecting them to cook properly, so I do it in stages. Give the pan another glug of olive oil and allow it to heat up, then add the onions with a big grind of salt. Cook the onions low and slow for about 30 minutes until soft and super-sweet. Add the meat back in and fry until the meat is hot again. Add the pul biber, oregano and sugar and allow the mixture to cool before using.

Preheat the oven to 400°F (200°C) and line a baking sheet with parchment paper.

Once each filo dough circle is stretched (see page 23), fold the dough from east to west, so you've got a rectangle lengthways. Fold the rectangle again, going from east to west. Add 1 tablespoon of the meat mixture to the base of the filo and form it into a flat square shape. We're looking to make a samosa shape with this one. Take one corner of pastry and fold it diagonally, so you've got a little triangle. Fold the point that's facing you up to overlap the already-folded pastry. You've now made 2 folds and you should be left with the same shape (triangle) you first started with. Repeat this folding process all the way to the top of the pastry rectangle. Repeat this with all the dough circles and meat mixture. It should make 10 cute little meat-filled böreks. Give the böreks a little egg wash before cooking them.

Stick them on the prepared baking sheet and bake for about 15 minutes until brown and crispy.

Çiğ köfte is a hard dish to explain. Yes, it's raw ground beef and raw bulgur, but the process cooks it, mostly from the heat in your hands and how much you have to knead it. I'm not gonna lie, this is a proper labor of love, however, the end results are worth it. It's no different to eating steak tartare and, in fact, I'd say tartare is more intimidating—at least this meat is hidden. You can smear it on lavaş or portion it. The main ingredient in Çiğ köfte is İsot (also known as Urfa biberi or pepper), which is basically pul biber but dried in the sun until it turns black. It's got a very distinctive flavor, sweet and earthy with a little background hum of heat, celebrated in the Anatolian regions of Türkiye. I don't often believe tales in food due to my limited imagination but, story has it, that the wife of a hunter created Çiğ köfte back when King Nimrod was in rule 3,000 years ago. The king prohibited cooking over fire, which led adventurous cooks to try new means. Yeah, ok man.

ÇIĞ KÖFTE Beef and bulgur köftes

- 1 lb (450 g) fine köftelik bulgur
- 5 tbsp pul biber
- 5 tbsp İsot (Urfa biberi)
- 1 lb 14 oz (850 g) good-quality beefsteak tomatoes, grated
- 3 garlic cloves, grated
- 1 tbsp acı biber salçasi (spicy pepper paste)
- 9 oz (250 g) lean ground beef
- 4 ice cubes
- scant ½ cup (100 ml) olive oil
- ⅔ cup (160 ml) pomegranate molasses, plus extra to serve
- 1 bunch of flat-leaf parsley, finely chopped
- 6 scallions, finely sliced
- sea salt and pepper
- lemon wedges, to serve

In a large tray, preferably circular with loads of working room, rub together the bulgur, pul biber and İsot. The bulgur should take on the color of the chile flakes and be an even color—this will take a couple of minutes.

Season the bulgur generously with salt and pepper and rub that through, too. Add the tomatoes, garlic and pepper paste. Bring this all together in the tray and knead it like you would a bread dough for about 30 minutes, squashing and spreading the mixture against the base of the tray. After 30 minutes, try a bit of the mixture—the bulgur shouldn't be as hard as raw bulgur.

Next, add the meat and keep kneading for another 30 minutes. After about 1 hour, the bulgur should be fully cooked and the meat and all the spices evenly spread. Add the ice cubes and knead until the mixture is cold to the touch. This is to stop the cooking process and help the mixture start to emulsify. Add the olive oil and the pomegranate molasses and, again, you guessed it, knead them in, too. This won't take that long, just make sure the mixture is all one color. Finish with the parsley and scallions and I promise this is the last time you'll mix it. Check the seasoning, it should be spicy, salty and meaty.

Grab a little handful of the mixture—about 1¼ oz (35 g)—and roll it into a sausage shape. Then squeeze it in your hand so the köfte takes on the grooves of your fingers to help it pick up any lemon juice or pomegranate molasses when you serve. Repeat with the remaining mixture and serve with lemon wedges and an extra drizzle of pomegranate molasses.

EF GF

SERVES 4

This is the first thing I ate in Istanbul, from a little lokanta selling loads of roast meats and vegetables. It's a little like a Subway—you choose what you want and they plate it up for you. Canteen-style steel railings and serving trays work down the line as people choose multiple dishes over rice. It's mostly aimed at cab drivers and late-night workers, somewhere to stop and get a home-cooked meal. I went with the chicken thighs and potatoes, got a little salad and was given a separate bag with a whole loaf of cut bread in it. I took it all home, stuck on Turkish TV and polished it off.

You can use chicken breasts for this recipe; just make sure they're on the bone, otherwise they'll be so dry you might choke. All you gotta do really is marinate the thighs. There are no tricks or little tips here, just put all those ingredients in the bowl and coat the chicken. If you really want to, you can marinate the chicken overnight, but I let it rest for just one hour and it was still delicious.

FIRINDA TAVUK One-pan roast chicken and veg

- 2 tbsp pul biber
- 2 tbsp full-fat thick yogurt
- ½ mug of vegetable or sunflower oil
- 1 tbsp tatlı biber salçasi (sweet pepper paste)
- 6 garlic cloves, grated
- 4 chicken thighs
- 4 chicken drumsticks

FOR THE ROASTING PAN

- 2 kapya peppers, roughly chopped
- 2 onions, quartered
- 4 Cyprus potatoes, peeled and cut into quarters
- 2 tomatoes, quartered
- 2 whole garlic bulbs
- olive oil, for drizzling
- sea salt and pepper

Mix the pul biber, yogurt, oil, tatlı biber salçasi and grated garlic together. Add the marinade to the chicken and give it a good massage for about 5 minutes, making sure you get the marinade under the skin and all over. Marinate in the fridge for a minimum of 1 hour and anywhere up to 3 days.

Preheat the oven to 425°F (220°C).

Once the chicken is marinated, add the peppers, onions, potatoes, tomatoes and garlic to a large roasting pan. I just cut these into the pan in my hand, keeping the size of each bit of veg uniform, otherwise you'll have onion dust and raw potatoes. Season all the vegetables with loads of salt and pepper. Season the chicken with salt and pepper and stick it in the pan. I try to make sure that the thighs are touching the base of the pan because they'll need more heat. It's fine for the drumsticks to be sat on top of the vegetables; they'll cook a lot quicker but it means they'll have more time to soften and fall off the bone. Add half a mug of water to the leftover marinade in the bowl and mix it in to make a bit of a sauce. Pour that all over the top to help the potatoes cook.

Give it another seasoning of salt and pepper and a couple of zigzags of olive oil and roast for about 1½ hours. Easy.

The most common pide is kuşbaşı, which translates as "bird's head" in reference to the size of the meat's cut. This is a really easy recipe. Mix it all together, use the dough from the Breakfast Pide recipe on page 140 and you're good to go.

KUŞBAŞILI PİDE Meat bread

- 1 lb (450 g) lean lamb
- 1½ cups (280 g) chopped tomatoes
- 6 oz (180 g) light green pointed peppers, deseeded and finely diced
- 1 bullet chile, deseeded and finely diced
- 2 kapya peppers, deseeded and finely diced
- ½ tsp smoked hot paprika
- 1 tsp cumin seeds, toasted and crushed
- 1 tsp pul biber
- 1 tsp acı biber salçasi (spicy pepper paste)
- 1 tbsp butter, plus extra to serve
- 3 tbsp oil
- 1 quantity of Breakfast pide dough (see page 140)
- sea salt and pepper

Cut the lean lamb into pieces about ¾ inch (2 cm) wide, then mix all the ingredients together, except the pide dough, seasoning with salt and pepper. It gets better the longer it sits but you can also use it straight away.

Preheat the oven to 475°F (240°C).

To shape the pides, divide the dough into 2 balls and roll one out into an oval shape. The main thing here is that we get more length in the dough than we do width, so roll the dough to about ¹⁄₁₆ inch (2 mm) thick. Add a good handful (about half) of the mixture down the middle, leaving about a 1 inch (2.5 cm) gap all the way round the edge. You don't need loads of mixture, you can spread it pretty thinly, otherwise the dough will cook before the filling does. Fold the dough around the outside inwards, towards the filling. Don't cover loads of the filling when doing this, but if there's a little underneath the flap, no drama. Do this on both sides and crimp together the ends. Repeat with the remaining dough and filling.

Transfer to a dry baking sheet and bake for 8–10 minutes, turning halfway through cooking. Once cooked, rub a little pat of butter around the crust and in the middle. Cut each pide into 4 pieces to serve.

EF GF

SERVES 5

Like I've said before, in Türkiye, "kebap" doesn't mean meat and sticks. The word refers to the cooking fuel—mangals with charcoal or wood-fired ovens for slow braising. I cooked this in my wood oven outside, which makes a massive difference; I like to do things the way I've seen them done, almost paying respect to the craftsmanship and the years that these recipes have been around. A lot of the dishes that I enjoyed on my travels I didn't really wanna fuck around with. I wanted to bring that experience and flavor back before bastardizing. I wanted to make sure that we as foodies, chefs and authors are actually celebrating the history. This doesn't mean that you can't do it in your oven at home, but my indoor oven is just a little bit shit.

Like the rest of the kebap recipes, this is a hand-chopped meat recipe, but if you can't be bothered, just get the butcher to grind you an entire rib. When hand-ground, the onions almost confit in the lamb's fat and it makes a huge difference. There are 25 onions in this recipe and I know that sounds excessive, but it'll feed five people easily, so consider this an alternative Sunday roast dinner. It doesn't need all-day cooking, just a big prep job.

GAZİANTEP KEBABI Grilled köfte and onions

- 2 lb 10 oz (1.2 kg) lamb rib meat, ground (see intro)
- 14 oz (400 g) lamb tail fat, ground
- 2 tbsp pul biber
- 4 garlic cloves, minced
- 25 white onions
- olive oil, for drizzling
- generous 2 cups (500 ml) meat stock (optional, see page 27 for homemade)
- a couple of long red peppers or chiles (optional)
- sea salt and pepper

FOR THE SAUCE

- 1 tbsp water
- 4 tbsp pomegranate molasses

Mix together the meat, fat, pul biber, garlic and a couple of good grinds of salt.

To prepare the onions, just take off the tops and the first layer of onion flesh as this doesn't cook down as well and can often be a bit tough. Cut all the onions in half down the middle. Season the cut sides with salt and pepper.

Preheat the oven to 375°F (190°C).

Take about 2 oz (60 g) of the meat mixture and form it into a little oblong. Sandwich it between 2 onion halves and place in a roasting pan. (I bought a 16 inch/40 cm diameter round roasting pan from the Turks for this.) Repeat with the remaining meat mixture and onions until you have no more space.

Zigzag over some olive oil and give it another touch of salt and pepper. I added a couple of ladles of stock to help the onions steam—nothing major, just like an eighth of the way up the pan. Cover the pan with parchment paper and foil. Bake in the oven for about 45 minutes. Remove the parchment paper and foil, mix together the water and the pomegranate molasses for the sauce and pour over the top. Add a couple of long red peppers or chiles over the top, if you like. Turn the oven up all the way (475°F/240°C) and roast for 15–20 minutes until the edges of the onions start to char and the meat takes on some color. Eat this with fresh bread, rice and yogurt.

EF GF

SERVES 4

I guess kavurma is similar to a ragù—it's beef braised in stock until it's soft. I like to reduce all my liquid off so it's almost like a Turkish pulled beef. Serve this with fasülye or pilav, or it's great with a couple of fried eggs and some toast.

There isn't really a specific cut of beef for this; you want something lean that breaks down, like a roasting joint. My butcher often has cubed beef in the window, so I just went with that. This is home food in Türkiye, so it wouldn't be made with rib eye or sirloin. It's something you'd come home to that Mom's made on a winter's night, with a roughly cut salad, beans or rice to follow.

KAVURMA Slow-cooked beef

vegetable oil, for frying
2 lb 4 oz (1 kg) lean beef, diced
10½ oz (300 g) white onions, finely diced
3 bay leaves
3¾ cups (900 ml) beef or chicken stock (see pages 26–27 for homemade)
1⅔ cups (400 ml) water
sea salt and pepper

Heat some vegetable oil in a wide frying pan until it's smoking. Season the beef heavily with salt, but don't add the pepper yet or it will burn and won't be fragrant. Seal the beef hard in the hot oil, giving it a good outer crust. The beef will release a lot of moisture into the pan, so keep the heat high until all the liquid has cooked off.

Once the liquid has evaporated and the beef begins to fry again, add the onions and cook them for 30 minutes until they're dark from the beef juices, soft and sweet. Add the bay leaves next and cover with half the stock. Reduce the stock until you're left with nearly no liquid. Add the remaining stock and repeat the process. The reason we're doing it twice is because we want the beef to take on as much flavor as possible.

Once the second batch of stock has cooked off, pour in the water, cover the pan with a lid and simmer for about 35 minutes until the meat starts to soften. Once the meat is soft to the touch and starts to break away, reduce all the water down until you're left with about half the liquid. Eat it as is or save it for the breakfast recipe on page 178.

GF

SERVES 4

I ate this in Diyarbakır in a tiny bustling breakfast spot full of locals, with waiters shouting out numbers of teas and how many guests for breakfast. The youngest waiter, who was probably about 11, was in charge of running up and down the street to get more bread from the bakery. This wasn't something special on the menu, this was just the way the eggs were served with every breakfast, and as soon as I ate it I was actually excited to make my own version.

KAVURMALI YUMURTA Slow-cooked beef and eggs

2 tbsp butter
olive oil, for frying
2 kapya peppers, deseeded and sliced
6 oz (180 g) Kavurma (see page 177)
2 red chiles, sliced
3 eggs
pinch of pul biber
sea salt

In a large frying pan, melt 1 tablespoon of the butter with about double the amount of olive oil. Fry your kapya peppers first, with a pinch of salt, until they're just starting to soften. Add the kavurma next and continue to cook.

Once the meat is hot, add the chiles and fry those just until they start to smell spicy. Crack the eggs into the pan and give them a little mix. Season with salt, stick the remaining butter on top and cover with a lid for a minute or so, just so the egg on top cooks. Finish the dish with the pul biber and you're good to go. Shout out to all the eggs.

Karakoca
20 cl
SOĞUK
İÇİNİZ
SUYU

EF GF

SERVES 4

Now that you've conquered the world of getting meat to stick to skewers and hand-chopping ground meat, let's change it up a little. Traditionally, alinazik is cubes of lamb, but when I had it in Gaziantep, where the dish originates, it was a beautiful skewer of köfte. As previously discussed with other dishes, it's traditionally made at home in Türkiye, but is considered more of a "special" in kebap shops abroad. I'm a little sick of cubes of meat on skewers as I've been eating them since I had teeth, so to see it done differently and alongside my new obsession with hand-chopped köftes, I decided why not mix the two together?

ALINAZIK Köfte with coal-roasted eggplant and yogurt

- 3 tbsp pul biber
- 1 quantity of köfte mixture (see page 176)
- 1 large eggplant
- ⅔ cup (150 g) full-fat thick yogurt, warmed gently in the microwave (see method)
- ½ garlic clove
- juice of ¼ lemon
- sea salt

FOR THE CHILE BUTTER

- ½ tbsp butter
- ¼ tsp acı toz biber

Add the pul biber to the köfte mixture, mix in and set aside.

For the eggplant, light the BBQ and get it spanking hot (see "How to Light a BBQ" on page 246). I don't bother piercing eggplants. Why would we make holes for the juices to escape when you're trying to trap the flavor inside? Over a 1 count, grill the eggplant on all sides until it's limp and soft to the touch. A lot of chefs neglect the end of the eggplant and end up with undercooked bits in their baba ghanoush, so make sure you grill the butt, too. Once the eggplant is fully cooked, set it aside in a bowl with a lid or covered in plastic wrap and allow it to cool down.

Once cool, cut the top off the eggplant and split it down the middle lengthways. The flesh closest to the charred skin is where all the flavor is, so although it looks dark you want to include that, too. Once you've got all the flesh out of the eggplant, chop it finely and return to the bowl it rested in. Don't waste any of those juices. Give the eggplant a grind of salt and a mix, then let it sit.

When it comes to Turkish recipes with yogurt, you wanna use the full-fat stuff, not Greek because it's a little too loose and doesn't have that punchy acid. If you have to use Greek that's fine, just don't microwave it. If you're using the full-fat stuff, you're gonna have to nuke it in the microwave for 10 seconds a time, just to loosen it. Grate in the garlic and add the lemon juice.

All we've gotta do now is make a chile butter. Melt the butter in a small pot and add the toz biber. If you do this beforehand it will set, so reheat as needed.

Over a 3 count, grill the köfte according to the instructions on page 176.

Let's build. Add your chopped eggplant to a flat-based bowl. Don't spread it thinly but let it live in the middle, then hide the eggplant with all the yogurt sauce and cover the remaining empty parts of the bowl, too. Pull off 2 skewers of köfte and break into little sausages. Place on top. Pour over the chile butter and let it bleed through the dish. Dip in some bread, if you like.

ADANA (Southern Türkiye)

By the time I reach Adana, I've eaten more kebaps than I thought ever existed. As I wander the streets, men skewer up red and green bullet chiles ready to serve to customers who have ordered something grilled wrapped in bread. Lamb-fat clouds fill the cobbled streets along the main strip. Mountains of charcoal spill out of shop garages which, commonly, people still cook over here. Sparks fly as cheap steel is welded together to make ocakbaşı. Oranges shine on fruitful trees under the 70°F winter sun—I'm still the only person wearing shorts.

As a city, Adana feels a little more modern: there is less of a focus on modesty as I can see women dressed like mainstream Europeans and spliff-smoking skater dudes in Atatürk Park. There's the odd Burger King or Chinese restaurant for students who don't wanna go home and eat Mom's food tonight. In the high-end fashion outlets here, you can buy real Nike sneakers. Building-tall palm trees along the roadside have made it feel a little like LA, including the people drinking iced coffees. It's a Westernized scene that I hadn't realized I'd been missing—I've been away for five and a half weeks now. I do miss London—even the crackheads and loud-mouthed kids.

Despite my yearning for some home comforts, I'm in Adana for one thing and one thing only: Adana kebap. I walk for an hour and a half to find a guy cooking Adana döner kebap over logs, who I'd discovered on YouTube. When I get there, he's closed. Disappointed and hungry, while stood outside what was supposed to be the best döner I was gonna eat, it slowly dawns on me that I've strayed a little too far from the main strip. The modernity and first impressions I got of Adana have faded—and that once comforting feeling of home has evaporated. I tried not to look over my shoulder on my way here, as I didn't want to draw attention to myself. But now I look over my shoulder, I realize I've been followed by a group of about ten guys who don't look that happy with me being there. I'm not scared, 'cause it's daylight, but I'm not too sure what my next move is gonna be. The only reason I walked all this way was because I couldn't find a cab to take me, so I'm pretty sure there isn't going to be one around to take me back. I need to assert a bit of dominance and know I can't look weak or crumble. I give the boys a head tilt; a gesture that isn't polite or impolite, but shows them I'm Turkish. As I walk closer, they give way to let me walk between them, looking me up and down like a piece of döner meat. I really don't want anyone to read this and be freaked out. This shit happens all over the world, it's not exclusive to Türkiye. I've been G-checked on nights out in pubs back in London, too—it is what it is. I walk back to the city center with the lads heckling me a bit. I can hear them talking about where I could be from and how big my sneakers are. I keep my cool, keep it moving and eventually manage to hail a cab out of there—the only one I've seen in about two hours.

In two days in Adana, I eat five Adana kebaps. Each a little different to the last, some fiery that make me sweat, others on the less fatty side, and a few with mint and pomegranate molasses in the salad. The algorithm often serves me videos of Turkish food on Instagram, mostly men doing shit over fire. But there's one guy in particular—short, with a square head and jaw—who's always squinting over intense coal heat and squashing Adana kebap on to bread while serving up 10 different salads. He's my first stop, at Yeşil Kapı Kebap. Ducking through a very small door, I immediately realize cleanliness is a bit of an issue, but it's heaving with locals, so I take this sign as a green light (unless, like me, this is the first time they've been here, too, and we're all just as worried about spending the rest of the day violently shitting ourselves). I get shown to a very small table. You know when you're in reception and you're sat at those plastic tables with big thick legs on a tiny little chair that fits underneath them? No joke—exactly the same height as that. I shoot a text in the boys group chat: "I'm sitting on the world's smallest chair in Adana. You lot would shit yourselves with laughter" along with a picture of my shin pressed against the lip of the table's surface. Nawaz shoots a dig at Hus for being short, implying this seating arrangement is perfect for him.

The Adana kebap arrives: two skewers of heavily spiced lamb sitting on top of stretched fluffy bread; stained with meat juice, still hissing from the heat. It's garnished very simply with two heavily blistered chiles that are waiting on a small, circular steel dish. Casual foreplay starts as I taste the salads and test the ezme to see where we're at—and if this lives up to the Insta showreels. Slow-roasted shallots, dressed in pul biber, sumac and pomegranate molasses, fight for space on a side plate among thinly shredded onions and parsley. The ezme is mostly tomato; tart with vinegar, fresh with tomato juice and clean with a peppery finish from good, home-pressed olive oil. My waiter delivers more seasoned bread, plonking it down directly on to the one-time-use, thin, paper tablecloth. I'm not given any silverware, but I don't question it—I'm no stranger to getting my hands dirty, and I reckon this'll be well worth it.

EF GF

SERVES 4

TAVUK ÇEVİRME

Corner-of-a-butcher's roast chicken and spices

Often in Türkiye, butchers will have rotisserie chicken spinning away in outdoor ovens, slowing cooking, waiting for people to take them home. I visited a butcher's shop with two little stools placed in the corner for people to sit and eat. With no food back at my accommodation, I decided to sit here and eat a whole rotisserie chicken on my own, almost barbarically, and with bare hands like my dad would. The chicken was served with little sachets of spicy Turkish ketchup along with a little bag of seasoning. The chicken skin was tight and crisp, the little sachet of seasoning almost felt like the type of seasoning you get in instant noodles. The chicken was cooked so well that it was barely holding together but still really soft and not dry. I managed to tuck away three-quarters of the chicken and fed the rest to the most adorable stray. The owner's wife was really cute and talkative and asked why and where I had come from. I confessed that I had seen a YouTuber eating in their butcher's and her face lit up with joy. We had a little chat about life over multiple cups of tea as she served customers chicken, cooked and raw.

Now, here we are—over halfway through my second cookbook. I've worked a couple of Hasan tricks and now I present to you: Corner-of-a-butcher's roast chicken and spices. I know this is a "rotisserie"-inspired recipe, but none of us actually have the facilities to make a rotating spit at home. For us normal folk, we just want to roast a bird in the oven.

Get chatting to your local butcher, build a relationship, then ask for their advice on the best bird they have for roasting. Good butchers aren't there to rip you off, a lot of them care about their products and will be happy to sell you something top quality in return for having you as a returning customer.

The secret to this recipe is using a dry brine and an organic bird. Dry brining is essentially salting the meat, which draws out the moisture, but also allows the bird to soak it all back in. So yes, we could just do salt and sugar brine, but this is our first opportunity to impart flavor—so let's make a little rub that will bring out the flavors in our mystery spice bag.

CONTINUES OVERLEAF

10 NUMARA ÇEKİLİŞE KATIL
1 kişiye
10 kişiye
calvekazandiriyor.com

1 x 4 lb (1.8 kg) whole organic chicken
12 tbsp (170 g) butter, at room temperature
olive oil, for drizzling
sea salt

FOR THE DRY BRINE

1 heaped tbsp soft light brown sugar
2 sprigs of rosemary
4 sprigs of thyme
1 tsp coriander seeds
1 tsp cumin seeds
3 tbsp sea salt
½ tsp black pepper
zest of 1 lime
zest of 1 lemon

FOR THE SPICE MIX

1 tsp dried oregano
1 tsp sweet paprika
1 tsp pul biber
1 tsp curry powder
½ tsp MSG
1 tsp sugar
½ tsp sea salt

TO SERVE

homemade fries (optional)
Turkish ketchup (optional, can be found in Turkish supermarkets or online)

Place all the dry brine ingredients, except the citrus zests, in a blender and whizz them together until the mixture is a fine, uniform consistency. Put the mixture into a bowl and stir through the lime and lemon zests. Set aside for later use.

In a small bowl, mix the spice mix ingredients together, then set aside until it's time to serve.

The chicken itself doesn't really need much prep—remove anything that's inside the cavity of the carcass, then separate the skin from the breast. Do this while the bird is whole; the same way you would when preparing a holiday turkey. Using half the dry brine mixture, rub it underneath the skin of the chicken breasts. Ensure that it's evenly coated, from the top to the bottom of the bird. Now do the same with the legs of the bird.

Rub the remaining dry brine over the outside layer of the bird's skin, spreading any leftovers inside the cavity, too. Let the bird brine in the fridge for at least 6 hours. For best results, it's an overnight job.

An important thing to ensure a delicious bird is allowing your chicken to come up to room temperature before cooking it—cold chicken always cooks unevenly. To avoid this, remove the brined chicken from the fridge 4 hours before cooking.

Once the chicken is up to room temperature, use a clean, dry tea towel to pat the chicken dry and brush away any brine left on the skin of the bird. Preheat the oven to 400°F (200°C).

The last chicken prep stage is spreading the butter under its skin. When you've spooned it between the layers, use your fingers to smooth out the butter evenly. Give the outside of the chicken's skin a splash of olive oil and sprinkle with a little salt.

Put the chicken in a roasting pan and place on the middle oven rack to roast. Don't open the door until 45 minutes have passed, then rotate the chicken and return it to the oven for a further 35 minutes of roasting. The chicken should just start to crisp and firm up. If cooking meat scares you like it does my sister Alev, invest in a Thermapen—poke the thermometer in the thigh, making sure it's not touching a bone. When cooked, the chicken should be at about 153°F (67°C), and once rested it will climb to 162–167°F (72–75°C).

When the chicken is golden and its skin is crispy, remove it from the oven and leave it to rest, uncovered, for at least 15 minutes. Before serving, return the chicken to the oven for 10 minutes at the same temperature, just to warm it through.

Carve the chicken on a serving platter, pouring its resting juices and any melted butter from the roasting pan over the top. I served this dish with homemade fries, Turkish ketchup and a small, heaped pile of the spice mix for dipping.

TAM MEVSİMİNDE
TOPLANAN DOMATESLER
Calvé
ACILI
KETÇAP

EF GF

SERVES 4

Street food in Istanbul is a competitive market: simit sellers, stuffed mussels, döner boys, men on boats selling balık ekmek, but every so often you'll see a man pushing around a big glass cupboard filled with steaming rice and chicken. You can't miss them in Istanbul: they're often ringing bells or shouting about their rice. One of the cheaper street foods, this humble little street food dish makes a great dinner. I like the fact that no matter where you go in the world, someone is eating a variation of the chicken and rice combo, and this version just happens to be the Turkish variation. Basic meat, carbs and butter.

I think this is one of the most eaten dishes in Türkiye—whether it's breakfast on the go, a speedy lunch, dinner that Mom made, or when you're drunk leaving a shit Turkish nightclub at 4am, the pilavcı guys are there to look after you.

TAVUKLU PİLAV Chicken, rice and chickpeas

- 1 mug of baldo, white basmati or sushi rice
- 1 x 3½–4 lb (1.6–1.8 kg) whole chicken
- 5 tbsp (70 g) butter
- 1 x 14 oz (400 g) jar chickpeas, drained
- pul biber (optional)
- sea salt and pepper

Measure out a big mug of rice—baldo, white basmati, whatever. Wash the rice until the water runs clear—don't fuck around here, proper washed rice makes a massive difference. Once the rice is washed, soak it in enough fresh cold water to cover for at least 30 minutes.

Stick your chicken in a large stock pot and cover with water. I make my stocks the way the Chinese make theirs; I always do a first boil and discard the water to get rid of any impurities or blood from the chicken. Bring the chicken to a boil, then remove from the heat and discard the water. Rinse the chicken under cold tap water and wash the stock pot. Stick the chicken back in the stock pot, cover with water again, this time adding 3 or so big pinches of salt. Bring the chicken to a boil, drop the heat to medium and simmer, uncovered, for 35–40 minutes. Make sure it's a simmer—don't boil the chicken, otherwise you'll just end up with flavorless fiber and all the good shit will be in your water.

Once the chicken is cooked, take it out of the water and that liquid left behind is a lazy man's chicken stock, not cooked for ages building flavor, just good clean light chicken-y water. Take out a mug and a half of liquid (the same mug you measured the rice with) and set it to one side. The rest of the "stock" you can keep for stocks and soups, but when you're writing a book, you'd be surprised how much shit is in your fridge and how little space you have, so mine ended up in the sink.

CONTINUES OVERLEAF

In your favorite rice-cooking pot (I'm pretty sure we've all got one of those, it's not just me), melt half the butter just until it starts to foam. Add the drained rice and gently fry it for a couple of minutes. Season with a couple of pinches of salt and cover with the reserved stock. Stick a lid on and bring to a rapid boil. Add the remaining butter and the chickpeas and put the lid back on. Transfer the pan to the smallest gas burner or the lowest heat setting you have and cook for 12 minutes. Once the timer has gone off, turn off the heat, lift the lid, get a free rice facial from the steam, and bring any rice around the sides of the pot to the middle. Cover the rice with a clean, dry tea towel or some paper towels and the lid and allow to steam until you're ready to eat it.

Finishing the chicken is pretty easy. Remove any skin and take all the meat from the bones, pulling the cooked chicken with your hands. I saw someone do this on Insta the other day with an electric hand mixer (you know those twin turbo ones your nan had when you were a kid?), which by the way I didn't think was cool, I thought "Who the fuck has an electric hand mixer any more?". Season the chicken with salt and pepper and set aside.

Once again, I'm a sucker for serving things exactly the way I was served them or similarly, so grab yourself a little bowl, like a handful-sized bowl, lay the chicken down first, mostly in the center but it doesn't matter if you fill the sides, then pack in your rice and turn it out on to the plate. Finish with a crack of black pepper, or a sprinkling of pul biber, if you like.

There are loads of slow braises in Türkiye and I was contemplating making Konya kebaps, specific to Konya in central Türkiye: whole lamb braised in lamb fat for hours and hours until it's soft and tender. But, realistically, when are you ever going to cook a whole lamb? So instead, I did some research and found kağıt kebap—kağıt meaning paper, and kebap. You can use any lamb on the bone for this—ribs, shoulders, legs—but I went with shanks. They comprise of three different muscles that are quite lean and tasty. Yeah, this is gonna cook for 5½ hours, but this is possibly the easiest kebap recipe of them all. No fuss and little effort, as the oven does all the work. For me it's the taste of Türkiye—glossy, salty lamb, simple veg for crunch and a bit of flat bread to mop it all up.

If you can't get lamb tail fat for this, ask the butcher for lamb fat, whatever they've got kicking about will work. Worst-case scenario, you can just use olive oil, BUT (and it's a big but) track down some tail fat if you can as it gives a completely different flavor.

KAĞIT KEBAP Paper kebap

- 10½ oz (300 g) lamb tail fat
- 6 lamb shanks on the bone
- 18 garlic cloves, unpeeled
- sea salt and pepper

Preheat the oven to 400°F (200°C).

Cut the fat into small cubes and stick it in a pot over low heat. Allow the fat to render; when the fat is fully rendered, the remains will start to go crispy. At that point, the fat is ready to go. Allow the fat to cool a little before using it.

If your lamb shanks are wet, which they often are, give them a good dry with a clean kitchen cloth. Season really heavily with sea salt and pepper, almost making a crust with the seasonings.

Cut 6 sheets of parchment paper big enough to wrap the shanks in. Scrunch the parchment paper into balls, then unscrunch, which makes it easier to work with. Stick 2 tablespoons of the tail fat into each piece of parchment paper, then add a lamb shank, plus a couple more tablespoons of tail fat over the top. I chucked in a few bits of the crispy tail fat, too and about 3 garlic cloves in each parcel. Wrap tightly with the paper, making sure there are no gaps for the oil to leak out. Stick the wrapped shanks in a roasting pan and pour any remaining rendered tail fat over the top of the paper parcels to stop them drying out.

Roast for 4 hours, then drop the temperature to 325°F (160°C) and roast for another 1½ hours.

I served mine with a couple of whole tomatoes and some long, hot green chiles. Any of the pilavs or salads in the book will work great, too.

MAKES 8 BURGERS

This is an Istanbul street-food classic. You'll see them dotted around in big glass boxes, stacked high and steaming away, often by tram or train stations that are open very early in the morning and super-late into the night. I ate one waiting for a boat from Beşiktaş. OK, I ate two. But they're small and damn good. You ever ordered a burger and let it steam in the bag for a bit? It's that but in the best way possible.

These are super-cheap, quick grab-and-go bites. It wasn't like the rest of the trip—I didn't go looking for the best islak burger, but I ate a good few. The best way to describe them is a sweet, soft burger bun with a punchy patty in the middle, covered in sauce. You can steam these in many different ways: in a bain-marie in the oven, on a plate in a pot, but the easiest way is dim sum steamer baskets. This is basically a Turkish bao bun. In Türkiye, it's usually just pretty standard soft rolls—however, I like the sweetness you get from brioche.

ISLAK BURGER Steamed burgers

- 1 lb 10 oz (750 g) ground beef
- 1 tbsp cumin seeds, toasted and crushed
- 2 tbsp pul biber
- 1 tsp freshly cracked black pepper
- 2 garlic cloves, minced
- 1 egg
- ⅔ cup (75 g) dried white breadcrumbs
- vegetable oil, for frying and greasing
- 8 brioche burger buns, halved
- sea salt

FOR THE ISLAK SAUCE

- 3 garlic cloves, finely sliced
- 1 x 14 oz (400 g) can plum tomatoes
- 6 tbsp tomato ketchup or Turkish ketchup
- 2 tbsp sugar
- 2 tbsp butter

For the burger patties, put the ground beef in a bowl, add the spices, black pepper, garlic, egg and breadcrumbs and mix for a good 5 minutes. For best results, let the meat mixture sit overnight in the fridge, but a couple of hours will do.

Shape the meat mixture into burger patties about 5 oz (140 g) each—we want the patties to be about ¾ inch (2 cm) thick. You should have 8 in total.

In a large frying pan, heat some veg oil over high heat until the pan starts to smoke. Season the patties on both sides with a grind of salt and cook hard and fast. Once they've developed a nice crust on one side, flip them and do the same on the other side. You don't have to cook the patties all the way through as the steam will finish them off. If you really want to, you can cook the meat off and steam everything together later. Set the patties aside.

Make the sauce in the same pan you cooked the patties, and using the same fat, gently fry off the garlic just until it starts to become fragrant and sticky. Add the canned tomatoes and break them down with a spoon. Fry the tomatoes for about 5 minutes, just until the water starts to evaporate. Fill the tomato can with boiling water and pour into the tomatoes. Stir in the ketchup, sugar and butter. Crank the heat to high and bring it to a boil, then remove from the heat.

Set up a steamer basket over a pot of boiling water. Make sure at least half the pot is filled with water so it doesn't completely evaporate. I've got 2 steamer basket layers, so I make the burgers 2 at a time. If you haven't got a steamer basket and you're going out to buy one, make sure you get the little sheets of paper that sit in the basket so the food doesn't stick. Oil the paper and lay

it in the steamer basket. Dunk the whole bottom half of the burger bun in the sauce and stick it in the basket. From there we're just gonna build our burger. Add the patty in next, with a couple of tablespoons of sauce over the top, and then dunk the top half of your burger bun in the sauce, too. Steam the burgers (in batches) for 6–8 minutes. The bread should be soft to the touch but still holding its form. If you want to eat them straight away, I recommend using a knife and fork, but if you're not a gluttonous bastard, wrap the burgers in parchment paper and let them cool for 10 minutes before eating them. After you've made them, you'll find yourself craving them.

MAKES ABOUT 10 SKEWERS/SERVES 5

I'd never seen this dish until I got to Urfa. Eggplants are usually a side, but why not make them star of the show? You'll need skinny eggplants; the big ones won't work as they won't cook in the same time as the meat and contain more moisture. You can find them in Asian or Middle Eastern supermarkets.

PATLICAN KEBABI Eggplant kebap

1 lb 14 oz (850 g) lamb rib, finely chopped
6 oz (170 g) lamb tail fat
2 tsp fine sea salt
6 oz (170 g) straight, skinny eggplants (not the fat ones), cut into 2 inch (5 cm) pieces

TO SERVE
lavaş
grilled peppers
grilled tomatoes
1 onion
chopped flat-leaf parsley

Although this recipe uses different measurements, follow the same steps as the other hand-chopped köfte recipes (see page 176) to make the meat mixture, mixing the ground lamb with the tail fat and salt as instructed.

To build your skewers, start with the eggplants and skewer a piece lengthways so we can grill it on all sides every time we turn it. Next, weigh up about 1½ oz (40 g) of your meat mixture, stick that on the skewer and try to shape it into a ball. I found it easier after adding the next piece of eggplant to almost secure it in place. Also, it's a lot easier to shape the mixture with a wet hand, as the water forms a barrier and stops the meat sticking to your hand. Repeat this process so you have 3 bits of meat and 4 bits of eggplant. You should have about 10 skewers in total.

Straight to the BBQ—you want a solid 2 count here and a constant flap to keep the heat up and the flames away (see page 246). With all the fat in the köfte meat mixture, if we try to cook them slow, the fat holding them together will melt away and they'll just fall apart, so you've gotta fire-roast these hard and fast.

Once the eggplant is soft and charred on the outside and the köftes are crispy on the outside and they've bellowed a lot of smoke for about 6 minutes, these are good to go.

To eat them, a little lavaş, grilled peppers, tomatoes, onion and some chopped parsley are all they really need. They should be smoky, the köftes should crumble with ease and the eggplant should have that deep wood varnish color once peeled. You don't have to peel the eggplants if you don't want to, but if they've cooked hard and fast and are a little burnt, you can.

This is an Urfa kebap I'd not seen before, not even on YouTube. We're using lamb loin to make it because it's lean, although leaner meats don't tend to do well on the BBQ as they dry out, so we're marinating it in milk for a day so it'll be nice and soft. For this recipe, you're gonna need a grill clamp so we have full control of the cook.

PİRZOLA Lamb loin kebap

2 lamb loin fillets
4 garlic cloves
1 tsp pul biber
1 tsp İsot (Urfa biberi)
sprinkle of dried flowering oregano
generous 1 cup (250 ml) milk
sea salt and pepper

FOR THE SECOND MARINADE

1 tbsp tatlı biber salçası (sweet pepper paste)
1 onion
5 garlic cloves
1 tsp pul biber
1 tsp İsot (Urfa biberi)
1 tsp cumin seeds, toasted and crushed
½ tsp kırmızı toz biber (Turkish paprika)
vegetable oil, to cover the mixture

TO SERVE

2 lavaş
grilled red chiles
grilled kapya peppers
grilled tomatoes
1 onion, quartered

Cut the lamb fillets into little finger-width medallions, then bash them out in between 2 pieces of parchment paper until they're about 1⁄16 inch (2 mm) thick. You can use anything heavy to do this—a rolling pin, a pestle or the mortar or a frying pan. Whatever you've got knocking around. Bash all the lamb out and stick it in a bowl. Now work on the marinade. Grate in the garlic, add in the pul biber, İsot and the flowering oregano and then finish off with the milk. The calcium in the milk helps to break down the enzymes in the lamb and make it super-soft. You can do this with buttermilk or yogurt, too. Give it a good mix, then cover and leave to marinate for at least 12 hours in the fridge, but for best results go for a full 24 hours. It makes a huge difference.

Once the lamb has been sitting in the milk for long enough, drain off any excess milk and discard it. There won't be loads as the meat will have sucked it up. Using a clean kitchen cloth, pat the lamb dry.

We're now gonna make a little rub to spread on the lamb before grilling. Add all the second marinade ingredients to a blender without the vegetable oil. Blend together until you have a smooth paste, then transfer it to a bowl, add the vegetable oil, just enough to cover the mixture, and don't mix it about too much. The oil is going to help create smoke on the BBQ and spread the marinade further.

Get the BBQ on a hard 2 count (see page 246).

Using your hands, spread the marinade along both sides of the lamb loins. Don't just dunk the meat in, we don't want loads. Rub a thin layer on with your fingers, place the meat into a grill clamp, making sure the meat isn't overlapping—touching is fine—we just want to make sure the meat has the opportunity to get a nice char. Close the grill clamp and season the meat on both sides. Grill the meat hard and fast for about 2 minutes on each side; I turned my meat over about every 30 seconds and I kept the heat up by flapping the charcoal. The last couple of flips I did, I laid a couple of sheets of lavaş across the clamp and pressed it on to the meat, picking up any juices or excess marinade.

To serve, I like to leave one of the lavaş on the bottom of the plate and stick the meat in the middle, then surround the edge of the plate with grilled red chiles, kapya peppers and tomatoes, and the onion.

07

DESSERT

GAZİANTEP (Southeastern Anatolia of Türkiye)

It's time for another four-hour bus journey—this time to Gaziantep. Bordering Syria, it's known for its Persian influence on Turkish food and is home to all things pistachio. I'm staying on the outskirts of Gaziantep next to a strip of new-build high-rise apartment buildings overlooking the densely populated city. Houses are built at different angles using every possible space available. A golden, misty sunset in Gaziantep feels almost Middle Eastern; from the light-brown houses and deserty slip roads that weave into the city center. Kids run around the backstreets playing soccer or zip around on scooters. Gaziantep is a beautiful ancient city. In the old market you can get anything: from gold and silver jewelry to hot food. There's soup, kebaps and steaming bread in abundance dressing the restaurant windows. Some women dress in traditional Syrian outfits, like modest belly dancers. They shop in groups while looking after their kids. Old men sit in the corner of market lanes, sharpening half-moon-shaped knives as Ottoman Empire flags hang above them.

I'm here almost a year to the date of the huge earthquake that devastated this part of Türkiye. I'm staying in a twenty-storey hotel which looks over remnants of the rubble. There are clear earthquake instructions on every door. There's an eery feeling, although that might just be my own trepidation. I'm a little nervous that Türkiye is still on the earthquake list, and I've also been getting safety warning emails saying to stay away from the Syrian border. To top it off, I wash my laundry in the hotel facilities and, instead of charging me 1,200 Turkish lira, they charge me 1,200 English pounds.

Despite all this, I'm excited to be deep in the heart of pistachio country. Gaziantep is where a lot of Turks believe that Turkish food originates. Antep is one of the larger culinary cities to visit in this region—with over 500 dishes originating here. It's also in the Top ten UNESCO list of cities to eat in—whatever the fuck that means. This is baklava and dessert country. I'm most excited to try katmer here, which is super-thin stretched filo, filled with sweet kaymak and pistachios. Crispy, good fat from waxy nuts and crunchy pastry.

I walk around Gaziantep, very full at this point with a fear of gout, looking for things I haven't tried before. At this point in my trip, I'm making very conscious decisions of what to eat. The first thing I do is seek out the covered market, which is slap bang in the middle of the city. I head into a little nut shop, where they're roasting pistachios in-house. The pistachios themselves are very different from the ones you get in the US or UK: bright purple skins, coated in dark rust-colored shells, warm, waxy and buttery. Grabbing a bag of double-roasted, extra-salted pistachios, I wander the streets trying not to leave a trail of shells—although most of them fall out of my pocket anyway. I look at guns in the gun shop, find some ridiculous spiked-kangal dog collars and watch men hand-beating copper pots—but the entire time my mind is on finding katmer… with warm crispy filo, creamy roasted pistachios and a glass of milk. It's 11am but I've been up since half past four getting everything together for my next bus trip. On vacation, that's a perfectly reasonable time to be eating dessert.

At the end of the market, I find the katmer place, which has people lining out the door. These guys just sell katmer—no baklava, nothing else—just trays and trays of pre-made katmer ready to be flashed in the oven. It smells almost like a French bakery, with softly caramelized edges of buttery filo in the air. Two heavy-shouldered men stand in a corner flying filo pastry over their heads to stretch the sheet, slapping it against the marble work surface then pulling until it's almost translucent. Trimming the filo into long rectangular shapes, they decorate it with fists full of sugar, pistachios, then a drizzle of melted butter.

I've discovered that traveling alone is largely great—but not so great when you go somewhere that only serves a portion that four people should share. Once again, I order for myself and am looked at like a complete BMI-dodger. My katmer comes out, cut into 16 little squares, with a log of mastic ice cream on the top with a little extra sprinkling of sugar and pistachios. A large glass of cold whole milk works as my chaser, because why not? Right? The filo crunches in between my back teeth, the ice cream coats the roof of my mouth, and the pistachios slowly grind into a paste. This shit is legit. I manage to tuck away three pieces before sticking it in a takeout box and giving it to a homeless man nearby. Worth the bus trip, worth the spinal arch I'm developing from the hang of my Türkiye belly. The trip to eat this dessert is a chef's dream.

I say it's a chef's dream... but by this point I'm struggling to get around and have to call it quits on day one of my eating tour around Gaziantep to hit the gym. Eighty lengths in the pool and a full stack on the bench press help. I head back up to my room to catch the sunset from my high-rise hotel. Opening the window (which I'd say defies health and safety regulations, opening dangerously too far) I have a little smoke and watch the sun set over the city. I can see how apartment buildings and tightly-placed houses are built at different angles to fill up any square inch of building space. Magpies circle high in figures of eight, with the evening call to prayer ringing in the streets.

When it's explained, künefe isn't something that sounds delicious. It's white string cheese cooked in shredded wheat with loads of butter and syrup, but that just doesn't do it justice. Crispy caramel notes from wheat cooked in butter, chew from cheap crappy mozzarella, sweet syrup to soak it all up. I feel like it's one of those desserts you don't ever forget, it's like a best friend you don't see that often, you don't have to speak to all the time, but when you're together shit's just normal and you feel like a better version of you. That's my good friend, künefe.

You can find fresh kadayıf (shredded filo pastry) in many international supermarkets, often vacuum-sealed in fridges next to the white cheeses. Worst-case scenario, there's always the frozen stuff. But fresh is always best.

To make proper künefe, you need a künefe dish—it's an aluminum plate but the base is dropped and it has a thick lip to help turn it. You'll need two of these.

KÜNEFE Cheese nest cake

- 3½ oz (100 g) kadayıf (shredded filo pastry), fresh if possible
- 9 tbsp (125 g) butter, plus extra at room temperature for greasing
- 2½ oz (70 g) mozzarella, sliced
- 8 tbsp lokma syrup (see page 212)

When you open the kadayıf, it will be in long strands. Using a pair of scissors, cut it into ½ inch (1 cm) pieces; it doesn't have to be precise, we just want to make it easier to work with.

Melt the butter in a saucepan, nothing special.

Mix the melted butter with the kadayıf using your fingers; don't squash it together otherwise it will clump. Smear a good thickish amount of butter in the first künefe dish. Press the kadayıf mixture into the dish. Add the mozzarella, trying to take up as much of the surface area as possible.

Scatter over the other half of the kadayıf dressed in the butter until you get to the top. Try to cover the mozzarella slices as much as possible so it doesn't melt through.

Over the smallest burner on a gas stovetop, cook the base of the künefe low and slow for about 15 minutes. I move it around the burner every 2 minutes so it's not taking all the heat from one spot. Künefe dishes are made out of cheap aluminum so they get hot real quick. At this point, we're cooking blind and need to use our other senses to help us get the crispy bottom we want. At no point should your künefe smoke. The smell of butter cooking should be in the air but not a caramel or brown butter smell and the edges should bubble—not crazy, but bubble. After about 5 minutes, the künefe will shrink ever so slightly, meaning that if you jolt the dish, the künefe will leave gaps around the edges.

You can have a little peek in those gaps to see how much color the künefe is taking on. I cook the künefe until the edges are starting to color, too.

Grease the other künefe dish with butter as before, then stick the greased dish on top of your künefe. This is where the thick lip comes in—you now have somewhere to hold when you flip it. Flip the künefe over in one quick move. Remember these dishes are gonna be super-hot, so use a couple of tea towels. The men in Türkiye who cook them in the street use 2 sets of pliers. Repeat the same cooking process on the other side, low and slow. The side you're now looking at should be golden, crispy and smell beautiful. If it's not, don't panic; if it needs longer, just cook the other side for longer, then flip it back. Don't do this before it's cooked though because it'll all fall apart.

Once cooked, spoon over the syrup, crank up the heat and give the syrup a quick boil. Once boiling, you're good to go. I let the künefe rest for a bit, before turning it out, otherwise you'll burn the living shit out of your mouth.

V

SERVES 4

This is a really simple dessert that I discovered in Trabzon, an area celebrated for its dairy. It's basically a sweet béchamel roux. I know that doesn't sound appetizing, but it's great. Promise.

SÜT HELVASI Turkish milk pudding

- 8 tbsp (120 g) butter
- 1 cup (120 g) all-purpose flour
- 6½ cups (1.55 liters) whole milk
- ½ cup (100 g) sugar
- 1 vanilla bean, seeds scraped out
- 1 egg yolk
- ⅓ cup (50 g) roasted hazelnuts, crushed (or crushed pistachios)

In a medium pot, warm the butter over low-medium heat until it's completely melted but catches no color. Turn the heat to low, then add the flour and stir to make a roux, which should take about 10 minutes.

When the flour has been cooked out, slowly whisk in 2¾ cups (650 ml) of the milk until the roux thickens to a smooth, silky consistency.

At this stage, stir in the sugar and the vanilla seeds, plus the whole pod after you've removed the seeds. Whisk in 2¾ cups (650 ml) of the milk and stir over low heat until the consistency is thick, like a béchamel sauce. This should take about 15 minutes.

Remove the pot from the heat and place on a heatproof mat. Stir in the remaining generous 1 cup (250 ml) of milk, then add the egg yolk and stir to mix.

Preheat the oven to 400°F (200°C).

Ladle the milky mixture into 4 ramekins or ovenproof clay pots. Bake in a bain-marie for 10 minutes until the milk has caramelized and is golden on top.

Remove the ramekins from the oven. Top with a sprinkling of crushed roasted hazelnuts. This also works well with a spoonful of jam or some poached fruit on top. You can leave süt helvası to set in the fridge for about 4 hours and eat cold later on or dig in now and enjoy warm.

EF GF V

SERVES 10

No one actually knows where Turkish Delight originates, but in the 9th century, cultures across the Arabian peninsula used rose water for beauty, religious, medicinal and culinary purposes. The Egyptians and the Ottomans also used it to cleanse themselves before meeting guests. I don't actually like the stuff, it tastes like aftershave.

I think it's safe to say we all enjoy ice cream, but who can actually be bothered to make it? But this no-churn condensed milk-rich ice cream is a cheater's method to get an easy smooth freeze. No ice cream machine needed.

DONDURMA Turkish delight ice cream

6 oz (180 g) pistachio Turkish delight
3½ oz (100 g) chocolate of your choice (milk, dark, bougie or crap)
4⅔ cups (1.1 liters) heavy cream
1¼ cups (14 oz) sweetened condensed milk

To be fair, this is just basically a mix together and freeze job. Chop the Turkish delight into little bite-sized pieces, they don't have to be uniform and perfect, but chop it to what you consider a reasonable amount to fit in one's mouth. If you want it chunky, go chunky. Do the same with the chocolate. I gave the chocolate the good old-fashioned cross-chop as if I was chopping herbs.

In a cold bowl, whip the heavy cream and condensed milk together until the mixture starts to stiffen—you want it to be firm and silky, like a good crème fraîche. If you dip your finger into the mixture, it should completely coat your finger with no drips, like acrylic paint. Use a stand mixer for this, as unless you go to the gym six days a week just to train your forearms, you'll be there a while.

Once it's come together, add the Turkish delight and chocolate. Fold it all carefully together with a spatula. Stick it in freezable plastic containers and freeze for at least 3 hours (it can then basically live in the freezer for a month or so). This mix will make a good 10 double scoops, so it's worth setting it in several containers.

Remove from the freezer about 45 minutes before you wanna serve. Scoop it out with a hot spoon to serve.

SERVES 4

Think Eton mess, but less private school and with a Turkish influence. This recipe is a lot like my life: just a little Turkish mess.

TURKISH MESS

1½ cups (250 g) pitted cherries, quartered
scant 1 cup (200 g) Greek yogurt
4 store-bought meringue cookies
scant ½ cup (50 g) pistachios, crushed
1 piece of dark chocolate

FOR THE CHERRY SYRUP
heaped 2 cups (250 g) cherries
3 tbsp sugar

FOR THE CHANTILLY CREAM
1 vanilla bean
2½ cups (600 ml) heavy cream
2 tbsp sugar

FOR THE FILO
5 sheets of store-bought filo pastry
3½ tbsp butter, melted
sugar, for sprinkling

To make the syrup, first pit the cherries. Now, as this is a syrup, don't worry about how prettily you're getting the pits out, just make sure they're out. Stick the cherries in a metal bowl and add the sugar. Cover the bowl with plastic wrap. Heat a small pot of water, which the base of the bowl can sit in without moving. You don't want the water touching the bowl, we just need the steam, like a bain-marie. Keep the water at a gentle boil. Leave the cherries to cook for at least 10 minutes. This is just a hack way of making a syrup without fucking around. I don't really do much dessert stuff, so I like to cut corners now and then. Once cooked, squash the cherries through a sieve, getting as much moisture out of them as possible. Don't throw away the cooked cherries, run a knife over them and set them to one side as we'll put them back in for a different texture.

Preheat the oven to 375°F (190°C).

Chantilly is just French and fancy speak for vanilla whipped cream. Scrape the seeds out of the vanilla bean. Stick the cream in a cold metal bowl, then add the sugar and the vanilla seeds. It helps if the bowl is cold because whisking creates heat and friction. I always make Chantilly by hand. You'll feel the cream start to stiffen—we're not looking for stiff peaks, tip-over-your-head-type stuff. Just cloudy and light cream, just holding together.

Brush both sides of each sheet of filo with butter, then scatter over some sugar; you don't need loads. Scrunch up the filo and stick it on a baking sheet. Bake in the oven for about 8 minutes until tanned and golden brown. Let the filo cool and then break it into more manageable shards.

Mix the fresh cherries with the syrup and cooked cherries. Then all you gotta do is basically build it. In 4 glass jars or mugs, layer the bottom with the cooked cherries and syrup, then stick a big tablespoon of the Chantilly and a big tablespoon of yogurt in each one. I like using the yogurt because it gives the dessert a little lift and acidity. Be generous with the cherry syrup when building to help cut through all the flavors. Crumble over some filo shards and meringue. Stick the pistachios on next. Keep repeating this until you run out of glass or ingredients. Top the mess with a couple or so more shards of filo and pistachios. Grate over the dark chocolate for a little color change and you're good to go.

Since going to Türkiye and having the real deal in the motherland, I got a bit of a reality check and realized the lokma in my first book weren't up to par. For those of you that don't know, lokma are made from fried batter, they're super-crispy and drenched in simple syrup. These are great for parties and birthdays and are super satisfying to eat, but one is never enough. Any leftover syrup can be used to make the künefe recipes on pages 206 and 228.

LOKMA (2.0) Syrup doughnuts

8 cups (1 kg) all-purpose flour
1 heaped tbsp superfine sugar
1 x ¼ oz (7 g) envelope fast-action instant yeast
pinch of salt
3¾ cups (900 ml) lukewarm water
any type of oil, for frying

FOR THE SYRUP
4 cups (800 g) sugar
3 cups (700 ml) water

Sift the flour into a large mixing bowl, add the sugar, yeast and salt and mix well. Pour in the lukewarm water and whisk together for about 3 minutes until the batter is smooth with no lumps. Cover with plastic wrap and allow the yeast to do its thing. The mixture can stand for at least 30 minutes; I left mine to rest at room temperature for 2 hours while I cracked on with other bits and it was fine.

The syrup is pretty straightforward. Add the sugar and water to a pot and bring to a boil, then drop the heat to low and allow it to simmer for 15 minutes. It won't be a super-thick syrup, so you don't have to cook it for ages. Once cooked, allow the syrup to cool.

The trick to getting good crispy lokma is actually the reverse of everything you know about frying. The first batch has to start in cold oil. This means that the lokma have a good amount of time to crisp and for the dough to cook on the inside. I usually use a Dutch oven or something pretty heavy duty with high sides to stop the oil from boiling over. You want to fry the lokma in at least 2 inches (5 cm) of oil, so there isn't really a liquid measurement—just make sure you've got enough to fry plus enough height on your pot for the oil not to spill.

Once the batter is ready, punch it back like you would a bread dough, to get any excess air bubbles out. Stick the pot of oil you're going to use over medium heat. Using a spoon coated in oil, pull out balls of the batter and place them into the oil. The easiest way to get equal-sized balls is to grab a fistful of batter, squash it in your hand and scoop what pops out between your index finger and thumb. A teaspoon will give you smaller balls and a tablespoon will give you whoppers.

Gently place the batter balls into the oil and allow the oil to slowly creep up to a frying temperature. Once the oil is hot enough, the lokma will float to the top; you want to fry them until both sides are super-crisp and a deep golden color.

Once the lokma are fried, dunk them into the syrup for 10 seconds and then stack them on a plate. The heat will hold in the lokma and, as long as you've cooked them long enough, they won't get soggy. Repeat the process until you're out of batter, but turn the heat down to low each time while you're scooping them in so they can creep back up to temperature again to crisp. Once cooked they'll keep for a day if covered at room temperature.

Here is a little something extra. Lokma are great as they are, but in Gaziantep they serve them dipped in chocolate, with a wedge of vanilla ice cream and cover them in crushed pistachios, which is game-changing.

The method and the cooking stays the same; the only thing that differs is that you need chocolate, crushed pistachios and cheap vanilla ice cream to serve.

Cook off all the lokma, melt 10½ oz (300 g) of your favorite chocolate in a metal mixing bowl over a pot of boiling water. Dump the lokma into the syrup, and then into the melted chocolate, toss them, stack them up, sprinkle over some crushed pistachios and serve them with ice cream. Fucking legit.

EF GF VG

MAKES 6 CUPS OF TEA

With Türkiye having the highest per capita tea consumers, it would be a shame not to give you guys a recipe. Way back, tea was used as a way to barter with the Chinese, almost as a currency. Now tea is grown in Rize on the eastern Black Sea, because of its mild climate and fertile soil. Tea is a very important drink to the Turks. Men gather in tea shops to smoke cigarettes, flick prayer beads and gossip. Turks are super-hospitable and there are little things that they do when it comes to caring for a customer, friend or family member that really shows the love: water on the table as soon as you sit at a restaurant, bread is always free, and leaving someone's house is almost impossible if you've not had tea. You'll always be offered it in a little glass cup. I'm not a massive hot drinks fan but when in Türkiye, do as the Turks do. The reason this tea is called Robert's tea is that my very good friend Robert takes his tea very seriously. Rob's a lover of all things Turkish and, while he used to have a degree in the art of rolling, he's more of a tea man now. I spent most of my nights off during my career at Deniz's (Robert's partner at the time) in North London with a joint, FIFA tournaments and enjoying takeout Chinese food. Rob's tea is special—warm notes of cinnamon and clove that Turks believe has healing qualities and take away any strong, dry bitterness. Rob pours them strong, no sugar, and to be fair, out of all the teas in Türkiye, nothing actually beats our Robert's.

You don't need a Turkish teapot for this, but I'm a man of tradition. You can get Turkish teapots easily online. Like an old-fashioned Italian coffee pot, Turkish teapots are two kettles stacked on top of each other. The bottom one is just to boil water, and the top one is to steep the tea leaves and keep them hot.

ÇAY Robert's tea

- 2 oz (60 g) loose-leaf black tea (Ceylon, if possible)
- 3 cinnamon sticks
- 2 tsp cloves
- sugar, to taste (optional)

Fill the base pot with water up to where the pot meets the spout and bring it to a boil. Add the tea leaves, cinnamon and cloves to the top teapot. Once the water is boiling, pour the water over the leaves, again up to about the spout. Refill the base teapot and bring to a boil with the tea leaves sat on top. Once the base pot comes to a boil, you're good to go.

Turkish tea is like a syrup and needs diluting. The liquid that the tea has steeped in will be strong and dark, so pour enough tea water into a mug or Turkish tea glass to fill it a third of the way up. Fill the rest of the glass with the boiling water from underneath. The more steeped tea leaf water you use, the stronger the tea will be. Add sugar, if you want it sweet. Turkish teas are a bit like Pringles, one just isn't enough.

This recipe will make multiple cups of tea for guests, plus the tea leaves and spices mixture can be used again over a couple of days, as long as you brew with fresh hot water.

Katmer is hands down my favorite dessert out of the filo bunch. It's creamy from the kaymak (Turkish clotted cream), but has a contrasting texture from the crunch of the pistachios. In Gaziantep, katmer is normally served with a glass of whole milk, but I like mine with ice cream.

GAZIANTEP KATMERI Sweet filo with pistachio

1 sheet of filo pastry (see page 23 for homemade)
2 tbsp pistachios, crushed, plus extra for serving
1 tbsp sugar
3 oz (80 g) krem kaymak or mascarpone
vanilla ice cream, to serve

Prepare your filo pastry according to the instructions on page 23. One sheet of filo makes one portion, so you can use any excess dough to make several servings, or for another recipe in this book.

Fold one piece of filo dough in half—from south to north. Fold the left and right hand sides of the filo inwards, so you're now working with a square shape.

Scatter the pistachios all over the square filo, then go in with a dusting of sugar.

Flick in the kaymak before folding each corner into the middle like a parcel, making sure each flap overlaps in the center, leaving no gaps.

Lift the katmer carefully into a flat roasting pan and bake at 475°F (240°C) until crispy and golden.

Serve with ice cream and extra pistachios.

This is a Turkish equivalent of the tres leches, that cake with three milks, caramel on top and a funny pattern. Anywhere you go for a dessert in Türkiye, you'll see huge trays of trileçe in the windows. Even if you walk around supermarkets, you'll find it in ready-made, just-add-milk forms. I've made a couple of tweaks and I think it's pretty good, to be fair.

TRILEÇE Milk and caramel cake

5 eggs
1⅔ cups (325 g) superfine sugar
3 cups (350 g) all-purpose flour
2½ tsp baking powder
2½ cups (600 ml) whole milk
1¼ cups (300 ml) heavy cream

FOR THE CHANTILLY CREAM
3¾ cups (900 ml) heavy cream
9 tbsp superfine sugar
1 vanilla bean, seeds scraped out

FOR THE CARAMEL
generous 1 cup (220 g) sugar
5 tbsp water
5 tbsp (70 g) butter, cubed
scant 1 cup (190 ml) heavy cream
small pinch of salt

Preheat the oven to 375°F (190°C). Line a baking dish with a lip with parchment paper; I used a Pyrex lasagne dish sized 16 x 11 inches (40 x 27 cm), which worked great.

Whisk the eggs and sugar together in a stand mixer until soft and fluffy; this will take a good 5 minutes until they've doubled in volume and the sugar has dissolved. Gently transfer the mixture into a big bowl with a spatula—we've spent all that time building air into our eggs and it would be a massive waste of time to now start smashing them around (I can be delicate, too). Sift in the flour and baking powder. Gently fold the mixture together until it's completely uniform. Make sure you're scraping the bottom of the bowl when folding so all the flour is in and combined. Pour the cake mixture into the prepared dish and give it a couple of gentle taps on the countertop to knock out any pockets of air for an even bake. Bake for 10 minutes, then turn the oven down to 340°F (170°C) and bake for a further 30 minutes.

Remove the cake from the oven and leave to rest until it's at room temperature. Take the cake out of the dish and peel off the parchment paper. Put the cake back into the dish, upside down, and using a skewer of some sort, poke loads of holes in the cake. Mix together the milk and the heavy cream and pour the liquid over the cake. I know this seems weird, just stick with me. The milky cream is going to give us a really soft, milky wet cake underneath. (If that doesn't sound delicious to you, don't bother making this.) Let the cake soak up the liquid; there will be excess but that's fine.

Chantilly is just the fancy French word for whipped cream. You can make this by hand (my preference) or in a stand mixer or with an electric hand mixer. Chantilly works best in cold bowls, so stick your bowl in the freezer beforehand. This is where reading the recipe before you start comes in handy. Please always read a recipe before you make it so you understand what you're working towards. It sounds self-explanatory but you'll be surprised how many people make recipes and forget what they've done by the end of them.

Pour the cream into the cold bowl, add the sugar and whip the cream just until it starts to stiffen. Then add the seeds from the vanilla bean and fold them through. A good Chantilly should be completely smooth, not sickly sweet and have enough density to hold a quenelle shape. Spread the Chantilly across the top of the cake. Stick the cake in the fridge for at least 1 hour so the cream has a chance to set before we add the caramel.

So far a piece of cake, right? Now for the dreaded caramel. Please be careful, this shit is hot and will burn you down to the bone if you get it on your skin.

Caramel is scary and doesn't work first time for everyone. Basically, in order to make a good caramel, you have to let it do its thing and trust the process. When cooking, we're all really fast to move things in pans, stir or shake handles. You can't do this with caramel, caramel is arrogant, it knows you wanna do all those things and if you do, the caramel will just decide to crystallize. You've gotta treat caramel with the utmost respect, you've almost gotta be a little scared while making it for it to work.

Weigh the sugar straight into a saucepan, making sure the pan is dry and clean. Pour the sugar into the center of the pan and try not to get any sugar up the sides. Add the water to a little jug or mug and pour it in gently, the sugar will suck up the water. Stick the saucepan over low heat, low-medium will do. Don't put this on your biggest burner and rush it. The sugar and the water will come up to a boil once the sugar has melted. Once there are no more sugar granules in the saucepan, then you can give it a little swirl once or twice, then no more. Stand over the caramel and watch it, the syrup will slowly start to change color around the edges and in the center. It will start to turn a light amber color, like the glasses your foreign nan had in the late 1980s or your white nan's Le Creuset. The color of the caramel will change quickly; we're looking at a deep copper color without the syrup smelling like it's burning. Reduce the heat and add the butter bit by bit. The caramel will react aggressively when the butter goes in, but that's fine, just stir it in with a big spoon so there's no chance of splash-back once all the butter is in. Remove from the heat before pouring in the cream and adding the salt. Allow to cool.

Once cooled to about room temperature, take the cake out of the fridge and pour the caramel over the top. Spread it evenly across the top in the same way we did with the cream.

Now, you can eat this straight away or stick it in the fridge for the caramel to set, too. If you let the caramel set in the fridge, you'll get a cleaner cross section when you cut it.

I know this sounds like an absolute long thing, but really, you've made a cake, whipped some cream and watched some sugar. It's worth every second.

MAKES 6–8 CRÊPES

I contemplated putting a baklava recipe in the book, but it's hard and takes years of understanding. Making my own baklava is like me going to Japan with no experience and writing a book about sushi. So, for now, here is a cheater's baklava using crêpes as the vessel. I had this in a little family-run dessert spot in Urfa. I was told by the waiter that şıllık tatlısı was a baklava they made using leftover lavaş, but I'm pretty sure he was chatting shit and it was just a crêpe. Possibly back in the day it would have been old lavaş, but there aren't really any loaves of bread in Urfa, it's all mostly flatbreads. Maybe it's the influence of the Middle East and Syria around the corner, but the change in bread types across my travels was very noticeable. Anyway, I'm rambling, but this is one of the best pancakes you'll ever eat, I promise.

ŞILLIK TATLISI Walnut-stuffed crêpes

2 eggs
1⅓ cups (320 ml) whole milk
1½ tbsp butter, melted, plus extra for frying
heaped 1 cup (140 g) all-purpose flour
pinch of salt
ice cream, to serve (optional)
ground pistachios, to serve (optional)

FOR THE SYRUP
2⅓ cups (470 g) sugar
2¼ cups (530 ml) water

FOR THE FILLING
2⅔ cups (300 g) walnut pieces
1 tbsp sugar

If you've got a crêpe pan, then great, but also if you're not an asshole with a fully equipped kitchen like me, then a large, wide-based frying pan will do just as well.

Crêpes are a piece of cake to make, all you've really gotta do is get the batter right. In a large mixing bowl, mix the eggs, milk and melted butter. Make sure the butter is melted but not hot; you should be able to put your finger in it.

Measure out the flour in another bowl and add the salt. Slowly whisk the wet ingredients into the dry—the batter will be kinda loose but that's fine, just make sure it's smooth. Let the batter rest for 20 minutes.

Like most desserts in Türkiye, this also has a syrup. Mix the sugar and water in a small pot, bring to a boil and simmer for 10 minutes. Remove from the heat and set aside.

To make the filling, pulse the walnuts in a food processor—it doesn't matter if they're still a bit chunky, we just don't want a powder. Mix the walnuts and the sugar together and set aside.

CONTINUES OVERLEAF

Heat a large, preferably nonstick, frying pan over medium heat, the lighter the frying pan, the better, as we want it to heat up quickly.

Melt a little pat of butter in the pan and stick a ladleful of the batter straight into the middle of the pan. Move the pan around in a circular motion to help the batter spread over the full surface of the pan; no matter what you do, the first one is always gonna be shit, unless you're Belgian. But use that as a guide to how much batter you need for it to work. The crêpe won't take that long to cook at all; once bubbles form in the batter and the edges start to pull away from your frying pan, have a little look underneath and see if it's starting to color. It doesn't need to be colored all over and a couple of leopard spots is enough. Flip the crêpe over and cook the same way on the other side—the crêpe will puff a little and have air pockets. That's fine, don't worry about it. The batter will make about 6 good crêpes and a couple of shit ones. When cooking the crêpes, stack them on top of each other and they'll stay warm.

When all the crêpes are cooked, fill them individually with about 1 tablespoon of the walnut mixture, like you're making a wrap. Roll them pretty tightly into long sausages. Transfer to a roasting pan with a lip and stick them on the stovetop over low heat. Once the pan comes up to temperature, pour over enough syrup to coat and let it rapidly boil for a couple of seconds. Any leftover syrup can be used to make the künefe recipes on pages 206 and 228.

You can serve them with ice cream and finish with ground pistachios. Fuck all that thirty-six layers of filo stuff, just make a crêpe, bro.

SERVES 8

I don't actually have a sweet tooth, although I'm aware I look like a man who would bleed some sort of syrupy substance. I don't often eat desserts out, nor do I make them at home. Desserts were present in my childhood, normally served by either my nan or a couple of aunties. White Janet's Baked Alaska was always a hit at Christmas, or Hala's Tel Kadayıf (crushed walnuts wrapped in shredded wheat) with a nice tea. More often than not though it was a piece of watermelon or a good old-fashioned Müller Yogurt Corner.

I think I neglected pastry because it's not my kind of cooking. Yeah, we should all know the basics as chefs: custards, meringues and tarts, but I wasn't and won't ever be a cook who geeks out or becomes obsessed with one thing in particular. I've got the other kind of ADHD, the type that's one step ahead, ambitious and stubborn and works better with grilling shit on the line. Successful pastry chefs are often wired different, comfortable working like a little troll in a quiet corner of the kitchen, not often giving out free offcuts and scribbling doctors' note-style ideas. However, I tilt my hat to them: in first, out last, creating food with multiple elements, most techniques painstakingly tested by some French dude 80 years ago. There's a lot of respect in that little, dark, great-smelling part of the kitchen.

Fuck all that though, here's a chocolate mousse recipe that works and it's bloody fantastic. I could have made up any old shit about my childhood and how aunties made me mousses whenever we went back home, but there's already a lot of blah in cookbooks. In no way, shape or form is this recipe authentically Turkish, but I noticed while away that Turks are fond of a good chocolate dessert, or anything drowned in Nutella. A lot of the mainstream restaurant dessert options in Türkiye are things covered in chocolate: chocolate-dipped strawberries, chocolate mosaic cake or chocolate pudding cups in jam jars. I serve this with a little dollop of kaymak, which you've already seen in the book. The kaymak has enough sourness to cut through the rich chocolate. This is therefore a "Turkish-inspired" recipe.

CHOCOLATE MOUSSE WITH KAYMAK

16 tbsp (225 g) butter, cubed
11¾ oz (340 g) chocolate of choice (I'd go for a nice dark one), roughly broken
5 eggs, separated
1 cup (200 g) sugar
pinch of sea salt

Stick the butter and chocolate in a large metal bowl and place over a bain-marie. For those of you who don't speak kitchen French, that's a pot of semi-boiling water. The bowl doesn't want to be touching the water, we're using the gentle steam heat. Keep the heat low and melt the butter and chocolate slowly.

While that's happening, we're gonna make a meringue and a sabayon. Sabayon is just the egg yolks, but the same principle. Add the egg yolks and ½ cup (100 g) of the sugar into a metal bowl and whisk until they're light in color and fluffy. You're gonna wanna use a stand mixer or an electric hand mixer for this,

FOR THE HONEYCOMB

1 heaped tsp baking soda
½ cup (100 g) sugar
3 tbsp golden syrup (or honey)

TO SERVE

krem kaymak or mascarpone
fresh raspberries

as doing it by hand is harder work. Whisk the yolks for 8–10 minutes until they are dull in color and tripled in volume. I know it sounds like an excessive amount of whisking, but we want to melt the sugar and create air. You'll know it's done when the mixture is smooth and the whisk leaves ribbons when you pull it out.

The meringues are a lot less work. Stick the egg whites into a stand mixer with ¼ cup (50 g) of the sugar to get the mixture going and give the sugar time to dissolve. Once the whites go from that frothy stage into the same consistency as the top of a cappuccino, add the remaining sugar and beat until you have soft peaks. Soft peaks mean that when you dip the whisk in and point it to the ceiling, the little drip should slowly curl in on itself but not break away. Be careful not to overwhisk the egg whites, as they can split. The consistency won't be uniform but like little grains that aren't totally smooth and pillowy.

Once the butter and chocolate have fully melted, add the sea salt to bring the flavors up. Let the chocolate settle for about 5 minutes so it's not really hot and the mixture doesn't scramble the eggs. Pour the butter and chocolate mixture over the sabayon first and whisk together. At first, it'll look like it won't come together and give you a muddy mixture. Make sure you're doing this with a Maurice or spatula, scraping the bottom of the bowl with every pass. Once it's all together, add half the meringue. Now it's very important that you're gentle here. I want you to fold in half the meringue, tilting the bowl on its side, scraping the side, scooping under, pulling the base to the top and repeating. Be dramatic with your movements but slow and consistent. Fold in the remaining meringue in the same way until the mousse is one consistent color. Now you can set the mousse into individual glasses or on a tray before refrigerating.

Honeycomb is a bitch, like most things you'll do when working with a caramel. The only way I've made honeycomb work is giving it my full attention and spotting little signs in the cook. I hope you guys get this right first time; it's a joy to make and watch. Before you do anything, line a high-sided roasting pan with parchment paper to avoid any spills and get your baking soda measured and in a ramekin.

Add the sugar and golden syrup to a deep-sided pot, stick it over medium heat and don't mix it until it's like 60% melted. Once the sugar has melted, stir the mixture pretty consistently, watching the edge of your pot—the edges will start to darken before the middle. Keep stirring until you get to a varnished wood color, not brown, not mahogany, but on the cusp of IKEA furnishings. Take the pot off the heat and let the caramel settle for about a minute, just for the bubbles to slow down.

Take the caramel to where your tray is lined, add the baking soda all at once and stir it in fast. Once all the baking soda is stirred in, pour the mixture into the roasting pan. The honeycomb will look a bit like high school science as it starts to grow—don't touch it, don't shake the tray, just leave it alone and let it cool completely.

Serve the mousse in glasses, or scoop quenelles on to plates, alongside a dollop of kaymak, broken honeycomb and some raspberries.

MAKES 1 /SERVES 4

Türkiye is one of the main exporters of pistachios, with the majority growing in Gaziantep. Pistachio trees flourish here because of the ideal climate. Usually harvested in September, pistachio harvesting is brought forward by one month if they are to be used for baklava because the fat content is lower and the protein count is high. Enjoy.

TAVADA KÜNEFE Cheese and pistachio nest cake

- ½ cup (55 g) whole shelled pistachios
- ⅓ cup (35 g) pistachios, crushed
- 2 oz (60 g) krem kaymak or mascarpone
- 2 tbsp butter, melted, plus extra at room temperature, for greasing
- 4 tbsp lokma syrup (see page 212), warmed
- ice cream, to serve (optional)
- ground pistachios, to serve (optional)

FOR THE KADAYIF

- 1½ oz (40 g) kadayıf (fresh if possible)
- ⅓ cup (30 g) ground pistachios

Stick the kadayıf in a bowl and give it a good chop with a pair of scissors so it's easier to work with. Add the ground pistachios and mix it all together, rubbing it between your hands. If you can't get ready-ground pistachios, stick whole ones—preferably unsalted—in a blender and try to get as much of the pistachio skin off the actual nut as you can. Give it a few quick blends, don't just let it rip or it'll turn into a paste. From here on it's just basically an assembly job.

Grease a künefe dish (see page 206) heavily with butter (you'll need 2 künefe dishes for this recipe). Add the whole pistachios, trying to get them as close together as possible and not leaving huge gaps. Sprinkle over the crushed pistachios, giving it a nice even layer. Flick in the kaymak, getting as much coverage as possible. If you just plonk the kaymak into the middle, you won't be able to spread it. Sprinkle over all the pistachio kadayıf.

Neaten the edges of the künefe and make it look pretty—give it a little press down, too. Pour the melted butter over the top.

Grease the second künefe dish you're going to turn the künefe into. Do not fucking rush it.

Now, unlike a regular künefe, you don't need to cook it for too long before flipping. Stick the künefe over low heat on the smallest burner on your stovetop and fry gently for about 3 minutes. We just want to toast the pistachios on the outside ever so slightly. Bringing them up to heat will help them let out their flavors through the oil.

Flip the künefe over into the second greased künefe dish and cook it on that side for 6–7 minutes, constantly moving the base so it's not taking too much heat in one part. Pour over the hot syrup while the dish is still over the heat and allow the syrup to boil for about 30 seconds

The kaymak in this gives you a creamier, lighter finish than the heavy string cheese in a normal künefe, so if you really wanted to you could serve this one with a dollop of ice cream. Finish with a sprinkling of ground pistachios.

I had a brainwave for a Turkish-flavored filling and these were the vessel. The pistachio cream is a nod to the flavors of Gaziantep, and the raspberry speaks to the English influences in my life. If you don't want to put the pistachio cream in, just raspberry jam is delicious, too. Also, just for the record, you can make a jam this way with just about any fruit, it's all the same principles.

RASPBERRY AND PISTACHIO DOUGHNUTS

⅓ cup (70 g) superfine sugar, plus extra for dusting
¾ cup (185 ml) whole milk
¾ oz (20 g) fresh yeast, or 1 tbsp (10 g) active dry yeast
3 tbsp butter
3 cups (350 g) bread flour, plus extra for dusting
small pinch of salt
2 egg yolks
sunflower or vegetable oil, for frying

FOR THE PISTACHIO WHITE CHOCOLATE CREAM
1⅓ cups (160 g) whole shelled pistachios
scant 1 cup (200 ml) whole milk
3¾ oz (110 g) white chocolate, chopped
2 tbsp butter

FOR THE JAM
1 lb 10 oz (750 g) fresh raspberries
juice of 1 lemon
3¾ cups (750 g) jam sugar (or regular sugar and boxed pectin; see method)

The dough is very similar to making a bread dough or a brioche. Start off by warming the sugar and the milk—it doesn't want to boil but needs to melt the sugar. While the milk is tepid, crumble the fresh yeast into a little bowl. Pour half the milk over the yeast and let it sit for at least 10 minutes to activate the yeast. Add the butter to the rest of the milk and let it melt.

Sift the flour into a bowl, then sprinkle in the salt. Add the egg yolks, yeast mixture and the milk. Bring the dough together with a wooden spoon; it will be on the wet side but that's fine. Tip the dough out on to a floured surface and give it a gentle knead for 5–8 minutes, just to help smooth it out. It doesn't need long, we don't want to overwork the gluten, otherwise we'll end up with tight, dense and heavy doughnuts; we just want light, airy and crisp. Stick the dough into a clean bowl, cover with a tea towel or plastic wrap, and leave the dough to proof at room temperature for at least 1½ hours until doubled in size.

While the dough is proofing, get on with the filling. Stick a pot of water over a high heat. Bring the water to a boil, throw in the pistachios and boil for about 4 minutes. Drain the pistachios and stick them into some cold water. Unfortunately, you're gonna have to peel the skins off the pistachios. Yes, I know it's a long process, but it's going to make the doughnut filling that much better. If you stick the pistachios in a large bowl of cold water, you can easily peel them under the water, instead of doing them one by one.

Stick the peeled pistachios on a clean tea towel and give them a good dry. Add the pistachios to a blender with scant ½ cup (100 ml) of the milk and blend until smooth-ish. Put the remaining milk and the white chocolate and butter in a metal bowl and melt over a bain-marie until fully combined. Once melted, stick it in the blender with the pistachios and blend until fully smooth and silky. Decant into a pastry bag and stick it in the fridge to cool.

You can use store-bought raspberry jam if you want, but when you make this and realize how easy it is and how much jam costs nowadays, you may be swayed. Start off by sticking 1 lb 5 oz (600 g) of the raspberries in a pot with the lemon juice. Set the pot over high heat and bring to a boil. Once the raspberries have broken down, transfer the mixture to a sieve and scrape it through. We just want to control how many seeds we end up with in our jam; a few are fine but loads will just get stuck in your teeth.

Stick the sieved mixture back into the cleaned pot with all the jam sugar (or sub regular sugar, and add pectin according to the instructions on your pectin package. You can do it without any pectin but your jam might be looser or take longer to gel.). Bring to a boil and let it boil for about 5 minutes. The way to check that your jam is cooked is by putting a tablespoon of it on to a plate and spreading it out to see what consistency it will be when it cools. If it's looking like jam, you're good to go; if it's more of a thick syrup, keep it boiling and check again. Once done, pour the jam out into a large bowl, add the remaining raspberries and stir them through. To get a long life out of your jam, sterilize some jars and fill 'em up and they'll keep in the fridge for months. Fill a pastry bag with the cooled raspberry jam and put it in the fridge.

Back to the dough. Once it has proofed, tip it out onto your worktop and give it a little spread with a rolling pin. Don't use too much pressure, just roll it over and stretch it out. You wanna keep the dough to the same size as a thick slice of bread. Use a circular cookie cutter, approximately 3 inches (8 cm) in diameter, to portion up the dough into 7–8 portions. Once portioned, let them proof again under a clean tea towel in a warm place for about 40 minutes. The portioned dough should have puffed up and be fluffy.

Heat enough oil in a deep, heavy-based pot to about 375°F (190°C). Basically, you want to make sure there's enough oil in the pot so the doughnuts don't sink and touch the bottom, so go biggest pot and at least 6¼ cups (1.5 liters) of oil. It's important to get the oil to the right temperature—not hot enough and the dough won't color fast enough and soak up the oil; too hot and the doughnuts will brown too fast and become bitter. Stick 2–3 doughnuts in the oil at a time, depending on the size of your pot—you don't want to overcrowd the pot as it will drop the temperature. Fry the doughnuts for about 4 minutes, turning them every minute. You'll know that they're done when you tap them with a spoon and they sound hollow. They should be a beautiful brown color, and light when you lift them out of the oil.

Once cooked, take the doughnuts out of the pot using a slotted spoon or sieve and drain on paper towels. Line a plate with superfine sugar and roll the hot doughnuts in the sugar until completely covered. Let the doughnuts rest for about 5 minutes before piping in the fillings; if the doughnuts are too warm, the filling will just spill out and all that hard work will be for nothing.

Make a small hole in a doughnut—it's best to do this round the middle that's a lighter color than the rest of the doughnut. Push the pastry bag three-quarters of the way into the doughnut and give it a good squeeze while pulling the pastry bag out. You should feel the doughnut expand and get heavier as you do this. Add the pistachio cream first, followed by the jam. Once they're all piped, you're good to go. If you've never made and eaten a fresh doughnut, you're in for a treat.

HOME FROM HOME (Northern Cyprus)

Leaving Adana, I was planning to move on to Mersin or Konya. But, as I try to book a single seat on the five-hour bus journey, the idea of being sat next to a stranger and being a stranger in yet another city feels exhausting... lugging the same suitcase around, packing up another round of laundry. I'm carrying my sneakers in my hand luggage at this point, running out of space because I've been buying seeds for my dad, magnets and lighters, stupid amounts of cigarettes and spices. I feel done. I've taken notes throughout the entire trip—a little mission control log where I've written out the recipes I want to make at home.

I don't know if it's just because of the palm trees, smiles and good weather I got in Adana, but I feel homesick; a funny homesick. It's not for home in London, it's for home in Cyprus.

With Adana being on the south coast and on the Mediterranean Sea, it's the closest I've been to Cyprus for about five years. I FaceTime Kamil (you'll never catch my dad with the phone by his ear, instead he'll always be shouting into the screen, peering down through his broken glasses): "Hello boy, you alright? Where are you now?," I spoke to Kamil in between Adana and Gaziantep, as he was helping with the £1,200 hotel cleaning bill fuck-up (see page 202), "What's up—your morale low?" My dad often notices when I'm battling depression or in the dumps, but he doesn't often ask me about it. "I'm alright man, I just miss home." "Come home then"—"I don't mean that home, I mean Eşref Villa."

When Kamil built our house in North Cyprus, on the same strip as his parents' house, he named it after his dad, Eşref. He told them, when leaving for the UK, he'd be back to build a house bigger than theirs next door and—fair play—he made it happen. When the rag trade was going well for Kamil in the late 1980s, the building he'd started was finished 13 years later when I was about five years old. He got a little etched plaque and stuck it to the brickwork outside. I remember, even then as a kid, my dad talking about the house with a big smile, pointing at the plaque and making sure we read it. He was a proud man. We're talking about a man who was born on a farm—who doesn't even know his birthday; only that he was born in March because his mom told him it was lambing season. A man who left school at seven to herd his dad's goats in the mountains. A man who was forced into a war. Although my dad's accomplishments are measured by being a foreigner in the UK (you know, that whole American Dream where a foreigner's achievements don't ever compete with that of someone who stays in their home country), but he's a man who's lived more life than most of us. I've inherited the same smile that my dad had when he was young; before he lost his parents, before his business wasn't doing too well, and before he lost almost all of his teeth.

Albeit on a very pixelated phone screen, and at an angle where I can mostly see nose and chin, Kamil looks the happiest I've seen him in a while as I announce my plan to fly to Cyprus. He tells me, "Just do it, boy." He often says to me in Turkish, when I'm questioning things in life, "Your house and family are waiting for you." Up until this point, I haven't thought about visiting my Cyprus home before. I hang up the phone and find a plane ticket for $50. I can't not do it.

I lay on my hotel bed crying—not out loud on some sad, black-and-white music video, knees-on-chin-in-the-bath thing—but just a lump in my throat, pressure in my chest and the odd, solo teardrop. I'm not describing it like that because I feel like I have to act tough. Men cry, and you should, too, once in a while, whatever it's over. It's good sometimes just to get rid of suppressed emotions, man. I'm just not a big crier and, like most men, bottle things up. I often let it turn into frustration or anger, then take it out on the wrong person or an asshole in a BMW. I try not to do this as much as I did in my teens, I am getting better at it, mostly through therapy and understanding. These tears are different, though. Cyprus has been on my mind since I touched down in Türkiye. In total, I've been away for six weeks. I've conversed with locals when I had to but have spent a lot of the trip in silence

with my own thoughts. I understand now why people do shit solo. Being alone with the personal monologue in my head has meant I've really had to listen to my emotions. I think it's a mixture of being homesick, exhaustion from traveling, fatigue from constantly being in work-mode every day and trying to be productive, or just knowing that I'm gonna be surrounded by loved ones and familiar faces soon—but the thought of coming home to Cyprus has really got to me. Like a closing chapter of this soul search.

I fill out my details on the Turkish Airlines app, wiping away tears so I can see the screen properly. I book the earliest flight out that arrives in Cyprus at 10am. I tell my cousins Nez and Afet. All the Cyprus family watch my moves on socials and know I'm in Türkiye. In our culture, it would be rude not to pop in. Even back in London, if I'm in your area or driving past, I'll drop in. My friends and family get it; it's a thing I've learned from them and carried on. The door to my house has always been very much open and it's very much still that way now. Growing up, our house was never empty—my cousin Refiye would be at ours after school and her dad would pick her up. Robert would drop in. Tre would come and knock for me. Aunties and uncles would pop in and out, almost every Friday. Julie Yenge would come over with Jelal and Asya. Uncle Vic would ring the doorbell, pulling off one leather glove as he waited for the door to open and taking off his hat before breaking the threshold. Esen Hala would come over with the girls. Grandma would come over with a freshly-baked Parkin, dressed to the nines in some new QVC Swag—everything color matched, down to the jewelry. Muharrem Amca would pop over to smoke four cigarettes, letting April run around the backyard with Denzil, then go. Hus will call me and say he's outside. I know this doesn't have much to do with my soul searching in Türkiye, but I've connected how it's a learned behavior of our culture and is always going to be a part of me. When Charlotte needed a place to stay, my family didn't even question it. When she moved in, Mom enjoyed having another woman in the house and Kamil got someone new that would read out his emails or buy him diabetes medication. Everything you know and love about me all stem from my mom and dad. Caring, providing and charming are all traits that I got from Kamil—he looked after whoever needed it. Happiness, humor, being allowed to be who I wanted, the want to nurture, a touch of OCD, smelling nice and being presentable are all things from Mom. My parents raised three strong-minded, hardworking, ambitious, individual kids with little else but love.

The next morning, after a 40-minute flight, I land at Ercan airport in North Cyprus. It's changed! It's no longer the bus shelter we used to arrive at as kids—there's neon signs advertizing casinos and nightclubs now. I rent a little zippy sporty Focus (classic red plate vacation rental), stick my charger in the aux, and line up the tunes I'm desperate to play out loud. I search for "Can't Hold We Down" by Kano ft. Popcaan, all windows down, singing the melodic intro over piano chords, "Man thankful, where I reach in life, man grow rough, ghetto youth we fight the fight, dem can't hold we now, can't hold we down." If you don't know this song or haven't seen the video, then you defnitely should. It's Kano and Popcaan having a BBQ with all their peoples. Kano's verse is reminiscent of what life was like for guys my age growing up in poorer parts of town: "We don't twist fingers and we don't wear bandanas; we just drink henny from the bottle, call it bad manners. Yeah, we're from bad manors." The sun's glaring off the road, my cheeks hurt from smiling and my throat's scratched from singing with bare passion; fingers glued in the compulsory gun finger signal. The motorway leads me into the green mountains with blue skies above; the deep blue lightening as it reaches eye level. A couple of bendy roads later as I break through the mountains, the road drops to the horizon. I'm home, man. Yeah, it's not North London but I'm welcome here. My people live here.

I pull up to the house and turn into the forecourt, just before the driveway. The terracotta roof almost gives it an East Asian vibe. Surrounded by hourglass-shaped pillars that make up the balcony, there's big sliding doors on the top floor. The balcony provides much-needed shade around the house, with huge, half-moon arches making up the veranda. The sharp edges and arches give the house a calming sharpness—like tough and rigid, but still inviting. The bottom floor balcony cuts off above a sharp drop into the garden. Fig, lemon and papaya trees grow in front of the house, with a lime and orange tree closer to the road. I open the gate and drag my bag along the entrance to the house. I open the door into the front room where me and Arif would play soccer indoors when it was too hot outside as kids. The house still smells like varnish from the dark brown staircase. It's peaceful.

I've never been here alone, but it's a house full of good memories. I think of my mom getting ready upstairs and smelling her hair, warm from the blow dryer. I think of Alev listening to the radio in her room. I think of Arif laying in front of the AC, legs crossed, throwing a ball in the air. I remember Dad showering in the backyard with a hose, repeatedly saying "this is the life, man" while scrubbing his face with a bar of soap. I can remember my nan calling my name from her balcony, telling me dinner's ready. I remember waking up early here, walking downstairs to see if my grandad was asleep outside or already out looking after the goats.

I jump back in the car and drive straight to Gulseren Hala's house. I don't want to say she's my favorite auntie (nor do I want to deny it), but she's done a lot for me in the past: let me stay at hers, fed me, cleaned up after me and taught me how to make helim. I pull into her driveway that leads into the back of her house, music thumping while beeping my horn. "Hala!," I call, knocking on her door. "Hasan... ?!." She gives me a big, warm, welcoming hug. I can feel her smiling. You know when you can just see the love in someone's eyes? "Did you give up on Türkiye? You done well to come here. I had a feeling that you were going to swing past. There's a plate of food for you in the kitchen. Let me cut a salad." She brings out a big plate of firin makerna (a recipe that you'll find in book one, *HOME*) plus a couple of bits of roast chicken, roast Cyprus potato wedges and a tomato salad full of scallions and fresh cilantro. "Come sit down, I've got bread, too." This is another new thing for me, I've never been to Cyprus on my own, or sat with family to have adult conversations. I guess when you're one of the younger ones, you always feel like the baby of the bunch. We sit and talk, crack a few jokes, as I share stories about my travels in Türkiye over a deep, grainy Turkish coffee. The empty feeling I developed after having miscellaneous conversations with cab drivers and kebap shop men has instantly gone. I'm safe, I'm secure and I'm loved.

With Dad being one of nine kids, it's hard to go to Cyprus and not see everyone. I hold the visits to aunties and uncles in high regard, the cousins not so much; it's an elder's thing. I'm not gonna go on and tell you about every interaction with my aunties and uncles in Cyprus, but the second stop is to Hasan Amca's, my dad's brother. Cyprus in February is still warm but, when the sun goes down, these dark-skinned islanders treat it like the Arctic; everyone rushes indoors, sticks on the heaters and gets under blankets. I drive up into the mountains to see Hasan, parking my car at the bottom of the marble steps and heading up to the gate yelling "Beh Hasan!" I hear movement from inside the house and my uncle say to his wife, "What is Arif doing here?" Hasan Amca isn't that mobile anymore, and a hip problem has left him with a walking stick. My auntie comes out of the front door—"Hasan, you won't believe it—it's Hasan!" "Which Hasan?" My auntie rolls her eyes to give me the universal sign of "you know what he's like" and tells him to get up to come and look. I'm met with the same warmth that he'd give his own son, "What are you doing here? What time did you get here?" I'm bombarded, in a nice way, with questions. "How's your mom and dad? Where's your girlfriend? How long are you here for?" and, the most important question of all, "Have you eaten?" My auntie makes phone calls to her kids, exclaiming "Little Hasan's here—come quick!" I sit with my auntie, uncle, their kids and my cousins for the rest of the day, eating little bits of homemade pickles.

I mean I guess that's what family is about, right? The security of being around people that share the same blood as you; the warmth of a smile, a genuine, caring question.

MASSEY FERGUSON 240 S

Although I've come to Cyprus to finish writing this book, I only have four days until I have to be back in Istanbul to fly home to London. Realistically, I know I'm not gonna write the introduction to the book, see the whole family and get a little break. So instead, I spend most of my time in Cyprus just being with family that I haven't been around in a while; the family that watch me from afar but care for me like I'm always there. The family that are just as proud of my success as my London-based family. All of my aunties and uncles make me feel like I have multiple parents, and it feels good knowing people have got you like that.

I spend four days dropping in on family with gifts and hellos from back home. I drive to Dipkarpaz to feed the wild donkeys and stroke goats—just to make myself happy. I cook for my cousin, Nez, and her husband, Mahmut, and their son, Rambo. I ask Rambo what he wants to eat, and he says he's seen me cook medium-rare steaks on YouTube, so that's what we do. I get us all a T-bone each, and Nez makes fries to make it a proper Cyprus dinner. We lost Sergul Hala, Nez's mom and my dad's sister, in 2016 to cancer. When we were kids on our six-week summer vacation, Sergul Hala would always be round at ours, or down the road at my nan and grandad's, making sandwiches to make sure we were all fed. She had a thick head of hair—a bit like mine—warm, soft, leathery skin, a cute mole on her face and a cheeky little smile. She was a strong, no-bullshit woman with a fierce energy. If I was gonna describe her in one way to anyone, it would be the female version of my dad. It was tough for the whole family when we lost Sergul Hala. It caused rifts between siblings and cousins. When she was diagnosed and we knew it was terminal, Arif, Alev and I decided to fly her out to London to surprise dad for his birthday in March and, again, it was one of those rare moments I saw genuine happiness from my dad. Later that year we lost her. There's always a special place in my heart for Nez, Sergul's daughter. She lived in London for about six years when I was in my teens. Nez would do anything for any of us, and she's checked in on me every day that I've been here—in the same way my mom and dad would if she was in London. I know I carry that torch along with her son, Rambo. I love that kid the way his nan loved me. Family is a bit like a curse, like a hex you're stuck with—but in a good way; an inherited piece of your history that you have to uphold.

I spend most evenings with Afet, my cousin who owns a hotel down the road. We drink negronis, smoke cigs and talk life. Afet's dad was my dad's Mom's brother and, when we lost Arif Dayı, the family hotel was left to her. Afet is a free spirit. She goes paddle boarding in the morning and drinks beers at night in between upholding a fully-functioning hotel with a cool bar. Although Afet grew up in Cyprus, I feel like she's the most Westernized. She didn't grow up with that village mentality and took herself away from it as soon as she could. She understands the relationship struggles I had with my dad, but also knows that he's my biggest fan. I don't have a book big enough to talk about everyone in detail. But what's important is that during these four days in Cyprus, they've all made time for me—they've all dropped in, offering to feed me—and, to be fair, it was the love that I was missing.

I guess if book one was dedicated to Mom, then book two has gotta be dedicated to Kamil; the little, brown, toothless tank. Cyprus' very own Robert De Niro. The trash-bag-dwelling, kebap-slinging, BBQ-in-all-weather expert. The half-job, wrong-tool-using handy man. (He recently leveled the stove with about £1.70 in change. Like, literal coins.) The man who would build you a house out of mud and sticks—it would be pretty shit, but he would give it a go. The man who's pretty funny, even when he's not trying to be. The man who mispronounces almost everything he says: "Play box," "bastami," "K4," "chicken tricky" (trick or treat), "kattypilar" (caterpillar) and "istirgram" (Instagram). The man who thought it would be really funny to shake every teacher's hand really hard at parents' evening. The man who insists on flying to Cyprus in a suit. The man who ate an entire pre-cooked chicken from Marks and Spencers in Gatwick airport with his bare hands. The man whose favorite parts of Christmas dinner are the beef and mustard, winding up Uncle Vic and reading out cracker jokes terribly. The man who, when his parents used to come over from Cyprus, would drive them to Alexandra Palace, walk up the hill and convince them you could see France in the distance. Large up Kamil, each and every time. Although we don't often see eye to eye, Kamil's taught me a lot. Pretty sure Kamil won't read this book, get any of the jokes, or agree with most things I've written. Although I never became a policeman like his golden boy, Arif—Arif can't make a proper omelet.

To be completely transparent: I love Kamil. Upon reflection, all I've ever wanted from Kamil is a pat on the back and not a sarcastic "well done." That's my old man; that's the man who brought me here. I think the older we get, we start to understand the paths our parents took to make shit happen. We clash because we're similar, as much as I hate to admit it. My dad was a war survivor and a prisoner. He fled his country and set up everything he could for us in the UK. It's a good feeling to have written a book about a culture that represents my upbringing, celebrates our differences—once a part of my identity that I steered away from. Yes, I didn't become a lawyer like the immigrant parent stereotype—but didn't end up in His Majesty's Prisons either. Although I don't think being a chef is the dream my dad had for me as kid, I like to think he's proud. Fuck it, I'm proud of me.

I feel like I've done a lot of growing up on this trip. I've been reliant on myself. Haven't relied on comforts, thrown myself in the deep end and have proven that I can do this food writing shit seriously. I'm not trying to prove it to you guys, more just to myself. Fuck your high school, fuck your university degree, fuck your perception of what an author should look like: don't ever settle for the category you're forced into. BUN THAT. GREATNESS ONLY.

HOW TO LIGHT A BBQ

Knowing how to properly light a BBQ arms you with all the basic science you need to understand how to maintain heat and be in control of your cooking.

To start your BBQ, begin by arranging the charcoal in a cone shape.

Stack pieces of charcoal about 7 inches (18 cm) high, layering larger and smaller pieces on top of each other. Leave some gaps between pieces to allow airflow, which is crucial for steady combustion. Fire needs fuel, ignition and airflow to thrive.

Once your cone is formed, light a small firelighter and place it into the opening at the top of your charcoal pile. Avoid moving it; let it ignite the charcoal gradually. Wait until the charcoal glows red all the way through—this ensures safe, even cooking and prevents undercooked food.

Cooking over live fire offers versatility. You can go low and slow or opt for high heat, depending on where you stack your coals and which part of the grill you use.

BBQ COUNTS

Throughout the book, you'll hear me refer to "counts" as this is how I was taught to measure the heat of a BBQ as a kid.

Stick your hand out over the fire, about 5 inches (13 cm) from the grill, and count to 5.

If you only get to a count of 1 before pulling your hand away in agony, that's a good temperature for charring veg.

A 2 count will cook fish super-fast and crispy (see page 80).

A 3-4 count is the optimum temperature for red meat and thicker-cut steaks; hot enough to get a good seal.

When cooking chicken, I always go for a 5 count, especially if you're cooking breasts.

GLOSSARY

acı biber salçasi | spicy pepper paste

acı toz biber | hot Turkish paprika, the hot version of kırmızı toz biber

baldo rice | grain that Italians use in risotto, but the Turks use as everyday rice

beyaz peynir | Turkish feta; crumbly, salty and sharp

Charleston salad peppers | long pointed light green peppers, usually used in salads

Corno di Toro (bull's horn) red peppers | long and pointy Italian peppers, great for roasting, grilling or eating raw. Richer in flavor than bell peppers. Easily available at most international grocery stores.

domates salçasi | tomato paste

gözleme | half-crispy, half-flimsy stuffed bread

İsot (Urfa biberi) | a type of chile grown in Türkiye, used mostly in the south that borders Syria. They are dried in the sun, crushed and then sun-dried again to give a darker characteristic flavor. Spicy but almost Mexican in flavor.

kadayıf | a batter that is pressed through a dial on to a hot plate, slowly rotated, cooking each little strand perfectly. Used mostly in desserts.

kapya pepper | the Turkish version of Corno di Toro peppers. Sweet long, and pointy.

kaşar peyniri | a Turkish household cheese made from sheep milk. When young and soft, it's like a Babybel, when matured, it's like a hard Cheddar.

kısırlık | a fine grain of bulgur usually served like couscous

Kaşkaval cheese | a hard village cheese, think of an aged Provolone

kırmızı toz biber| Turkish paprika

krem kaymak | Turkish clotted cream

Lebanese or Persian cucumbers | little stumpy cucumbers with less water for more crunch

pul biber | a somewhat spicy Turkish dried chile, coming in various heats and moisture levels. The stuff you'll get in most supermarkets will have a little hum but nothing crazy (also called Aleppo pepper).

sivri biber (green peppers) | long, skinny dark green pointy peppers that are mild in flavor and normally roasted in kebap shops

somun ekmek | loaf of bread

sucuk | spiced Turkish breakfast sausage (sometimes called sujuk)

sumac | a dried, powdered berry that's used across the Middle East to add sour notes to stews and salads

tatlı biber salçası | sweet pepper paste

tel (çeçil) peyniri | a string cheese from Southeastern Türkiye

INDEX

A
acı biber turşusu (pickled chiles) 29
Adana 36, 142, 182–3
Adana börek (cheese-filled filo) 132–3
Adana tost (toasted Adana sandwich) 142
Akçaabat köftesi 167
alinazik (köfte with coal-roasted eggplant and yogurt) 180
artichokes (enginar) 62–5
atom (yogurt-dressed peppers) 66

B
balık dürüm (new-school mackerel wrap) 82
balık ekmek (mackerel sandwich) 80–1
balık kağıt kebabı (cod in parchment) 94–5
balık köftesi (fish köfte) 88–91
balık şiş (Trabzon fish shish) 96–7
BBQ lighting and counts 162–4, 246
beans
  enginar (artichokes) 62–5
  piyaz (white bean salad) 48
beef
  Akçaabat köftesi 167
  çiğ köfte (beef and bulgur köftes) 172
  Gaziantep kebabi (grilled köfte and onions)) 176
  islak burger (steamed burgers) 194–5
  karniyarik (stuffed eggplants) 124–5
  kavurmalı yumurta (slow-cooked beef and eggs) 178
  kavurma (slow-cooked beef) 177
beet
  pancar ve beyaz peynir (beet, feta and pistachios) 34
  Yenge'nin pancari (Auntie Yenge's beets) 68–70
börek
  Adana börek (cheese-filled filo) 132–3
  börek (mixed meat pastries) 170
  sigara böreği (rolled cheese fingers) 110
bread
  Adana tost (toasted Adana sandwich) 142
  balık dürüm (new-school mackerel wrap) 82
  balık ekmek (mackerel sandwich) 80–1
  gözleme (filled flatbread) 144–7
  islak burger (steamed burgers) 194–5
  katmer (layered butter flatbreads) 150
  kuşbaşılı pide (meat bread) 175
  lahmacun (meat flatbread) 148–9
  Ramazan pidesi (Ramadan bread) 154–5
  sucuklu yumurtalı pide (breakfast pide) 140–1
  sütlü ekmek (milk flatbreads) 151
breakfast, Turkish (kahvalti) 108
bulgur
  çiğ köfte (beef and bulgur köftes) 172
  kısır (bulgur salad) 50–1
burgers: islak burger (steamed burgers) 194–5
butter, homemade 24–5

C
cabbage
  karişik turşu (mixed pickles) 29
  lahana turşu (pickled red cabbage) 60
cakes: trileçe (milk and caramel cake) 220–1
calamari 84–6
carrots
  enginar (artichokes) 62–5
  et suyu (meat stock) 27
  havuç tarator (carrot, yogurt and walnuts) 42
  karişik turşu (mixed pickles) 29
  mercimek çorbası (red lentil soup) 120
  mevlevi pilav (rice with carrots, pine nuts and walnuts) 121–3
tavuk suyu (chicken stock) 26
çay (Robert's tea) 216
celery
  et suyu (meat stock) 27
  tavuk suyu (chicken stock) 26
  tavuk çevirme (corner-of-a-butcher's roast chicken and spices) 184–6
cheese
  Adana börek (cheese-filled filo) 132–3
  Adana tost (toasted Adana sandwich) 142
  gözleme (filled flatbread) 144–7
  haydari ("hung" yogurt and walnuts) 40
  künefe (cheese nest cake) 206–7
  kuymak (breakfast cheese and polenta) 112
  peynirli mücver (zucchini, feta and corn fritters) 126
  pancar ve beyaz peynir (beet, feta and pistachios) 34
  sigara böreği (rolled cheese fingers) 110
  sucuklu yumurtalı pide (breakfast pide) 140–1
  tavada künefe (cheese and pistachio nest cake) 228
  types 247
  Yenge'nin pancari (Auntie Yenge's beets) 68–70
cherries: Turkish mess 210
chicken
  tavuk çevirme (corner-of-a-butcher's roast chicken and spices) 184–6
  et suyu (meat stock) 27
  firinda tavuk (one-pan roast chicken and veg) 174
  tavuk suyu (chicken stock) 26
  tavuklu pilav (chicken, rice and chickpeas) 188–91
  terbiyesiz tavuk (rude chicken) 162–4
chickpeas
  classic hummus 46
  salatalı humus (hummus with chopped salad) 47
  tavuklu pilav (chicken, rice and chickpeas) 188–91
chiles 247
  acı biber turşusu (pickled chiles) 29
  atom (yogurt-dressed peppers) 66
  ezme (Turkish salsa) 61
  Gaziantep kebabi (grilled köfte and onions) 176
  izgara ezme (grilled ezme) 44
  karişik turşu (mixed pickles) 29
  kavurmalı yumurta (slow-cooked beef and eggs) 178
  kuşbaşılı pide (meat bread) 175
  muhammara (pepper and walnut dip) 41
chocolate
  chocolate mousse with kaymak 226–7
  dondurma (Turkish delight ice cream) 209
  raspberry and pistachio doughnuts 230–1
  Turkish mess 210
çiğ köfte (beef and bulgur köftes) 172
cod: balık kağıt kebabı (cod in parchment) 94–5
condensed milk: dondurma (Turkish delight ice cream) 209
corn
  peynirli mücver (zucchini, feta and corn fritters) 126
  közlenmiş süt mısır (grilled street corn) 127
cream
  dondurma (Turkish delight ice cream) 209
  trileçe (milk and caramel cake) 220–1
  Turkish mess 210
crêpes, walnut-stuffed (şıllık tatlısı) 222–5
cucumbers 247
  ezme (Turkish salsa) 61
  Gaziantep salata (wet salad) 38
  salatalı humus (hummus with chopped salad) 47
  izgara ezme (grilled ezme) 44
  karişik turşu (mixed pickles) 29
  salatalık turşu (cucumber pickles) 28
cumin 166
Cyprus 232–44

D
dill: haydari ("hung" yogurt and walnuts) 40
dips
  atom (yogurt-dressed peppers) 66
  dip for calamari 84–6
  havuç tarator (carrot, yogurt and walnuts) 42
  haydari ("hung" yogurt and walnuts) 40
  muhammara (pepper and walnut dip) 41
Diyarbakır 136–9
dondurma (Turkish delight ice cream) 209
doughnuts
  lokma (2.0) (syrup doughnuts) 212–15

raspberry and pistachio 230–1
drinks
çay (Robert's tea) 216
rakı 33, 42
vişne 61

E
eggs
Adana tost (toasted Adana sandwich) 142
kavurmalı yumurta (slow-cooked beef and eggs) 178
menemen (tomato and pepper scrambled eggs) 114
peynirli mücver (zucchini, feta and corn fritters) 126
omlet (Turkish omelet) 115
sucuklu yumurtalı pide (breakfast pide) 140–1
eggplants
alınazik (köfte with coal-roasted eggplant and yogurt) 180
karniyarik (stuffed eggplants) 124–5
köpoğlu (eggplant, peppers and garlic yogurt) 54–7
patlıcan kebabı (eggplant kebap) 196
enginar (artichokes) 62–5
et suyu (meat stock) 27
ezme (Turkish salsa) 61
izgara ezme (grilled ezme) 44

F
fava beans: enginar (artichokes) 62–5
fennel
balık kağıt kebabı (cod in parchment) 94–5
et suyu (meat stock) 27
feta
gözleme (filled flatbread) 144–7
haydari ("hung" yogurt and walnuts) 40
peynirli mücver (zucchini, feta and corn fritters) 126
pancar ve beyaz peynir (beet, feta and pistachios) 34
Yenge'nin pancari (Auntie Yenge's beets) 68–70
filo pastry (yufka) 23
Adana börek (cheese-filled filo) 132–3
börek (mixed meat pastries) 170
Gaziantep katmeri (sweet filo with pistachio) 218
sigara böreği (rolled cheese fingers) 110
Turkish mess 210
firinda tavuk (one-pan roast chicken and veg) 174
fish
balık dürüm (new-school mackerel wrap) 82
balık ekmek (mackerel sandwich) 80–1
balık kağıt kebabı (cod in parchment) 94–5
balık köftesi (fish köfte) 88–91
balık şiş (Trabzon fish shish) 96–7
kalkan (Kumkapı turbot) 92

G
Gaziantep 202–5
Gaziantep katmeri (sweet filo with pistachio) 202–5, 218
Gaziantep kebabi (grilled köfte and onions) 176
Gaziantep salata (wet salad) 38
gözleme (filled flatbread) 144–7

H
haddock
balık köftesi (fish köfte) 88–91
balık şiş (Trabzon fish shish) 96–7
havuç tarator (carrot, yogurt and walnuts) 42
haydari ("hung" yogurt and walnuts) 40
hazelnuts: süt helvası (Turkish milk pudding) 208
hummus
classic hummus 46
salatalı humus (hummus with chopped salad) 47
kırmızı mercimekli humus (red lentil hummus) 47

I
ice cream: dondurma (Turkish delight ice cream) 209
iç pılav (Turkish rice with nuts and raisins) 22
islak burger (steamed burgers) 194–5
Istanbul 6, 16–19, 32–3, 74
izgara ezme (grilled ezme) 44
izgara kalamar (grilled squid with flowering oregano and pul biber) 98–101

K
kadayıf 247
künefe (cheese nest cake) 206–7
tavada künefe (cheese and pistachio nest cake) 228
kağıt kebap (paper kebap) 192
kahvalti (Turkish breakfast) 108
kalkan (Kumkapı turbot) 92
karişik turşu (mixed pickles) 29
karniyarik (stuffed eggplants) 124–5
katmer
Gaziantep katmeri (sweet filo with pistachio) 202–5, 218
katmer (layered butter flatbreads) 150
kavrulmus soğan (roasted shallots) 58
kavurmalı yumurta (slow-cooked beef and eggs) 178
kavurma (slow-cooked beef) 177
kebaps 161, 182–3
balık kağıt kebabı (cod in parchment) 94–5
Gaziantep kebabi (grilled köfte and onions) 176
kağıt kebap (paper kebap) 192
kavrulmus soğan (roasted shallots) 58
patlıcan kebabı (eggplant kebap) 196
pirzola (lamb loin kebap) 198
soğan kebabi (onion kebap) 168
kısır (bulgur salad) 50–1
köftes 161
Akçaabat köftesi 167
alinazik (köfte with coal-roasted eggplant and yogurt) 180
balık köftesi (fish köfte) 88–91
çiğ köfte (beef and bulgur köftes) 172
köftes (Turkish meatballs) 166
köpoğlu (eggplant, peppers and garlic yogurt) 54–7
közlenmiş süt mısır (grilled street corn) 127
Kumkapı 74
kalkan (Kumkapı turbot) 92
künefe (cheese nest cake) 206–7
kuşbaşılı pide (meat bread) 175
kuymak (breakfast cheese and polenta) 112

L
lahana turşu (pickled red cabbage) 60
lahmacun (meat flatbread) 136–9, 148–9
lamb see also tail fat
Akçaabat köftesi 167
alinazik (köfte with coal-roasted eggplant and yogurt) 180
et suyu (meat stock) 27
börek (mixed meat pastries) 170
Gaziantep kebabi (grilled köfte and onions) 176
gözleme (filled flatbread) 144–7
kağıt kebap (paper kebap) 192
köftes (Turkish meatballs) 166
kuşbaşılı pide (meat bread) 175
lahmacun (meat flatbread) 148–9
patlıcan kebabı (eggplant kebap) 196
pirzola (lamb loin kebap) 198
soğan kebabi (onion kebap) 168
leeks: tavuk suyu (chicken stock) 26
lemons
balık dürüm (new-school mackerel wrap) 82
balık ekmek (mackerel sandwich) 80–1
balık köftesi (fish köfte) 88–91
tavuk çevirme (corner-of-a-butcher's roast chicken and spices) 184–6
classic hummus 46
dip for calamari 84–6
enginar (artichokes) 62–5
ezme (Turkish salsa) 61
gözleme (filled flatbread) 144–7
salatalı humus (hummus with chopped salad) 47
izgara ezme (grilled ezme) 44
kırmızı mercimekli humus (red lentil hummus) 47
piyaz (white bean salad) 48
lentils
mercimek çorbası (red lentil soup) 120
kırmızı mercimekli humus (red lentil hummus) 47
lettuce
balık dürüm (new-school mackerel wrap) 82
balık ekmek (mackerel sandwich) 80–1
Gaziantep salata (wet salad) 38
piyaz (white bean salad) 48
limes: tavuk çevirme (corner-of-a-butcher's roast chicken and spices) 184–6
lokma (2.0) (syrup doughnuts) 212–15

M
mackerel
balık dürüm (new-school mackerel wrap) 82

balık ekmek (mackerel sandwich) 80–1
mangal 162–4
menemen (tomato and pepper scrambled eggs) 114
mercimek çorbası (red lentil soup) 120
kırmızı mercimekli humus (red lentil hummus) 47
meringues: Turkish mess 210
mevlevi pilav (rice with carrots, pine nuts and walnuts) 121–3
midye dolma (stuffed mussels) 76–9
milk
  pirzola (lamb loin kebap) 198
  süt helvası (Turkish milk pudding) 208
  közlenmiş süt mısır (grilled street corn) 127
  sütlü ekmek (milk flatbreads) 151
  terbiyesiz tavuk (rude chicken) 162–4
  trileçe (milk and caramel cake) 220–1
mint
  balık dürüm (new-school mackerel wrap) 82
  Gaziantep salata (wet salad) 38
  salatalı humus (hummus with chopped salad) 47
  izgara ezme (grilled ezme) 44
  kısır (bulgur salad) 50–1
  soğan dolmasi (stuffed onions) 130–1
  peynirli mücver (zucchini, feta and corn fritters) 126
muhammara (pepper and walnut dip) 41
mussels, stuffed 76–9

N
nuts
  Gaziantep katmeri (sweet filo with pistachio) 218
  havuç tarator (carrot, yogurt and walnuts) 42
  haydari ("hung" yogurt and walnuts) 40
  iç pılav (Turkish rice with nuts and raisins) 22
  mevlevi pilav (rice with carrots, pine nuts and walnuts) 121–3
  muhammara (pepper and walnut dip) 41
  pancar ve beyaz peynir (beet, feta and pistachios) 34
  raspberry and pistachio doughnuts 230–1
  şıllık tatlısı (walnut-stuffed crêpes) 222–5
  süt helvası (Turkish milk pudding) 208
  tavada künefe (cheese and pistachio nest cake) 228
  Turkish mess 210

O
olives: balık kağıt kebabı (cod in parchment) 94–5
omlet (Turkish omelet) 115
onions
  Akçaabat köftesi 167
  balık dürüm (new-school mackerel wrap) 82
  balık ekmek (mackerel sandwich) 80–1
  balık kağıt kebabı (cod in parchment) 94–5
  et suyu (meat stock) 27
  firinda tavuk (one-pan roast chicken and veg) 174
  Gaziantep kebabi (grilled köfte and onions) 176
  gözleme (filled flatbread) 144–7
  salatalı humus (hummus with chopped salad) 47
  iç pılav (Turkish rice with nuts and raisins) 22
  karniyarik (stuffed eggplants) 124–5
  kavrulmus soğan (roasted shallots) 58
  kavurma (slow-cooked beef) 177
  kısır (bulgur salad) 50–1
  köftes (Turkish meatballs) 166
  lahmacun (meat flatbread) 148–9
  menemen (tomato and pepper scrambled eggs) 114
  mercimek çorbası (red lentil soup) 120
  mevlevi pilav (rice with carrots, pine nuts and walnuts) 121–3
  midye dolma (stuffed mussels) 76–9
  piyaz (white bean salad) 48
  soğan dolmasi (stuffed onions) 130–1
  soğan kebabi (onion kebap) 168
  soğan salatası (Adana onions) 36
  tavuk suyu (chicken stock) 26

P
pancar ve beyaz peynir (beet, feta and pistachios) 34
patlıcan kebabı (eggplant kebap) 160, 196
peppers 247
  atom (yogurt-dressed peppers) 66
  balık kağıt kebabı (cod in parchment) 94–5
  balık şiş (Trabzon fish shish) 96–7
  ezme (Turkish salsa) 61
  firinda tavuk (one-pan roast chicken and veg) 174
  Gaziantep kebabi (grilled köfte and onions) 176
  Gaziantep salata (wet salad) 38
  izgara ezme (grilled ezme) 44
  karniyarik (stuffed eggplants) 124–5
  kavurmalı yumurta (slow-cooked beef and eggs) 178
  kısır (bulgur salad) 50–1
  köpoğlu (eggplant, peppers and garlic yogurt) 54–7
  kuşbaşılı pide (meat bread) 175
  lahmacun (meat flatbread) 148–9
  menemen (tomato and pepper scrambled eggs) 114
  muhammara (pepper and walnut dip) 41
pickles
  acı biber turşusu (pickled chiles) 29
  balık ekmek (mackerel sandwich) 80–1
  karişik turşu (mixed pickles) 29
  lahana turşusu (pickled red cabbage) 60
  salatalık turşu (cucumber pickles) 28
pide
  kuşbaşılı pide (meat bread) 175
  Ramazan pidesi (Ramadan bread) 154–5
  sucuklu yumurtalı pide (breakfast pide) 140–1
pilav
  iç pılav (Turkish rice with nuts and raisins) 22
  mevlevi pilav (rice with carrots, pine nuts and walnuts) 121–3
  şehriyeli pilav (everyday rice) 20–1
  tavuklu pilav (chicken, rice and chickpeas) 188–91
pine nuts
  iç pılav (Turkish rice with nuts and raisins) 22
  mevlevi pilav (rice with carrots, pine nuts and walnuts) 121–3
pirzola (lamb loin kebap) 198
pistachios 202
  Gaziantep katmeri (sweet filo with pistachio) 218
  pancar ve beyaz peynir (beet, feta and pistachios) 34
  raspberry and pistachio doughnuts 230–1
  süt helvası (Turkish milk pudding) 208
  tavada künefe (cheese and pistachio nest cake) 228
  Turkish mess 210
piyaz (white bean salad) 48
polenta
  calamari 84–6
  kuymak (breakfast cheese and polenta) 112
pomegranate molasses
  çiğ köfte (beef and bulgur köftes) 172
  ezme (Turkish salsa) 61
  Gaziantep kebabi (grilled köfte and onions) 176
  Gaziantep salata (wet salad) 38
  izgara ezme (grilled ezme) 44
  kavrulmus soğan (roasted shallots) 58
  kısır (bulgur salad) 50–1
  muhammara (pepper and walnut dip) 41
  pancar ve beyaz peynir (beet, feta and pistachios) 34
  soğan dolmasi (stuffed onions) 130–1
  soğan kebabi (onion kebap) 168
potatoes
  firinda tavuk (one-pan roast chicken and veg) 174
  gözleme (filled flatbread) 144–7
  mercimek çorbası (red lentil soup) 120

R
raisins
  iç pılav (Turkish rice with nuts and raisins) 22
  mevlevi pilav (rice with carrots, pine nuts and walnuts) 121–3
rakı 33, 42
  balık kağıt kebabı (cod in parchment) 94–5
Ramazan pidesi (Ramadan bread) 154–5
raspberry and pistachio doughnuts 230–1
rice 247
  iç pılav (Turkish rice with nuts and raisins) 22

mevlevi pilav (rice with carrots, pine nuts and walnuts) 121–3
midye dolma (stuffed mussels) 76–9
şehriyeli pilav (everyday rice) 20–1
soğan dolmasi (stuffed onions) 130–1
tavuklu pilav (chicken, rice and chickpeas) 188–91
rude chicken (terbiyesiz tavuk) 162–4

S

salads
ezme (Turkish salsa) 61
Gaziantep salata (wet salad) 38
kısır (bulgur salad) 50–1
piyaz (white bean salad) 48
salmon
balık köftesi (fish köfte) 88–91
balık şiş (Trabzon fish shish) 96–7
sausages see sucuk
scallions
balık köftesi (fish köfte) 88–91
çiğ köfte (beef and bulgur köftes) 172
ezme (Turkish salsa) 61
izgara ezme (grilled ezme) 44
kısır (bulgur salad) 50–1
peynirli mücver (zucchini, feta and corn fritters) 126
Yenge'nin pancari (Auntie Yenge's beets) 68–70
seafood
balık köftesi (fish köfte) 88–91
calamari 84–6
şehriyeli pilav (everyday rice) 20–1
shallots
izgara ezme (grilled ezme) 44
kavrulmus soğan (roasted shallots) 58
soğan dolmasi (stuffed onions) 130–1
soğan kebabi (onion kebap) 168
shrimp: balık köftesi (fish köfte) 88–91
sigara böreği (rolled cheese fingers) 110
şıllık tatlısı (walnut-stuffed crêpes) 222–5
soğan dolmasi (stuffed onions) 130–1
soğan kebabi (onion kebap) 168
soğan salatası (Adana onions) 36
soups: mercimek çorbası (red lentil soup) 120
soy sauce 160
balık dürüm (new-school mackerel wrap) 82
terbiyesiz tavuk (rude chicken) 162–4
spinach: gözleme (filled flatbread) 144–7
stuffed mussels 76–9
squid
calamari 84–6
izgara kalamar (grilled squid with flowering oregano and pul biber) 98–101
stocks
et suyu (meat stock) 27
tavuk suyu (chicken stock) 26
sucuk 247
Adana tost (toasted Adana sandwich) 142
menemen (tomato and pepper scrambled eggs) 114
sucuklu yumurtalı pide (breakfast pide) 140–1
süt helvası (Turkish milk pudding) 208
sütlü ekmek (milk flatbreads) 151

T

tavada künefe (cheese and pistachio nest cake) 228
tahini
classic hummus 46
kırmızı mercimekli humus (red lentil hummus) 47
tail fat
Akçaabat köftesi 167
balık köftesi (fish köfte) 88–91
Gaziantep kebabi (grilled köfte and onions) 176
kağıt kebap (paper kebap) 192
patlıcan kebabı (eggplant kebap) 196
tavuk suyu (chicken stock) 26
tavuklu pilav (chicken, rice and chickpeas) 188–91
tea: çay (Robert's tea) 216
terbiyesiz tavuk (rude chicken) 160, 161, 162–4
tereyaği (homemade butter) 24–5
tomatoes
Adana tost (toasted Adana sandwich) 142
balık kağıt kebabı (cod in parchment) 94–5
balık şiş (Trabzon fish shish) 96–7
çiğ köfte (beef and bulgur köftes) 172
firinda tavuk (one-pan roast chicken and veg) 174
Gaziantep salata (wet salad) 38
gözleme (filled flatbread) 144–7
salatalı humus (hummus with chopped salad) 47
islak burger (steamed burgers) 194–5
izgara ezme (grilled ezme) 44
karniyarik (stuffed eggplants) 124–5
kısır (bulgur salad) 50–1
köpoğlu (eggplant, peppers and garlic yogurt) 54–7
lahmacun (meat flatbread) 148–9
menemen (tomato and pepper scrambled eggs) 114
muhammara (pepper and walnut dip) 41
piyaz (white bean salad) 48
soğan dolmasi (stuffed onions) 130–1
Yenge'nin pancari (Auntie Yenge's beets) 68–70
Trabzon 104–7
balık şiş (Trabzon fish shish) 96–7
trileçe (milk and caramel cake) 220–1
turbot 74
kalkan (Kumkapı turbot) 92
Turkish breakfast (kahvalti) 108
Turkish delight ice cream (dondurma) 209
Turkish ketchup
Adana tost (toasted Adana sandwich) 142
tavuk çevirme (corner-of-a-butcher's roast chicken and spices) 184–6
islak burger (steamed burgers) 194–5
Turkish mess 210
turşu
acı biber turşusu (pickled chiles) 29
karişik turşu (mixed pickles) 29
lahana turşu (pickled red cabbage) 60
salatalık turşu (cucumber pickles) 28

U

Urfa 158–61

V

vermicelli: şehriyeli pilav (everyday rice) 20–1
vişne 61

W

walnuts
havuç tarator (carrot, yogurt and walnuts) 42
haydari ("hung" yogurt and walnuts) 40
mevlevi pilav (rice with carrots, pine nuts and walnuts) 121–3
muhammara (pepper and walnut dip) 41
şıllık tatlısı (walnut-stuffed crêpes) 222–5

Y

Yenge'nin pancari (Auntie Yenge's beets) 68–70
yogurt
alinazik (köfte with coal-roasted eggplant and yogurt) 180
atom (yogurt-dressed peppers) 66
dip for calamari 84–6
firinda tavuk (one-pan roast chicken and veg) 174
havuç tarator (carrot, yogurt and walnuts) 42
haydari ("hung" yogurt and walnuts) 40
köpoğlu (eggplant, peppers and garlic yogurt) 54–7
pancar ve beyaz peynir (beet, feta and pistachios) 34
Turkish mess 210
yufka (filo pastry) 23
Adana börek (cheese-filled filo) 132–3
börek (mixed meat pastries) 170
Gaziantep katmeri (sweet filo with pistachio) 218
sigara böreği (rolled cheese fingers) 110
Turkish mess 210

Z

zucchini: peynirli mücver (zucchini, feta and corn fritters) 126

ACKNOWLEDGMENTS

Big up the team at Pavilion. Ellen, for purely putting up with my shit and letting her hair down with my family in Cyprus. Laura, for letting me do pretty much whatever I want, and believing I could pull a book out of my ass with a very quick turnaround.

Large up Liz and Max each and every time—for another beautiful book, looking after me on shoots, Liz for constant smiles and Max for taking me out on my birthday while we were away in Türkiye. Love you guys.

Big up Mom for only semi-complaining this time about how much kitchen mess I made. I'll be out of your hair soon when my second album goes multi-platinum. Love you.

Charlo, for always believing in me. For bigging me up all the time, putting up with my strops and holding it down while I was away.

Arif and Esin, for running around for me on shoot days in Cyprus and getting to eat great food in return. You're welcome.

Alev and Oli, for coming over and eating the new recipes and being my biggest fans. Love you guys.

To all the aunties and uncles in Cyprus that opened their doors to me and the team. Thank you.

Afet, for looking after (and pretty much over-feeding the crew) the entire time.

Nez, for always being there for us and being a sister to us all.

Grace and Frankie, for being the people I talk to almost every day. You got me from the start, made it happen, put me in the right rooms with the right people. Thank you for not only being my agents but being my fucking dargs.

To the mandem, always. For checking in, making sure I wasn't dead. This is for all of us ❤️

Until next time guys.
Love always.

Thanks.

AUTHOR BIO

Hasan Semay is a half Turkish Cypriot half British chef, YouTube and Instagram sensation, as well as a self-confessed "proper North Londoner." Has was accepted onto the prestigious Jamie Oliver "15" TV show in 2011 and his relaxed and informative approach to cooking without pretentiousness has won him legions of fans over on his YouTube platform, *Sunday Sessions*. His debut cookbook, *Big Has: HOME* is a *Sunday Times* Bestseller. In 2023, Has became a judge on BBC3's *Young MasterChef*.

Praise for *Smoke and Seasoned Bread*:

"Jam-packed full of incredible food from his travels around Türkiye, this is Hasan at his best—bold, honest, beautiful, and full of heart."—**Jamie Oliver**

"Propulsive, evocative and spilling over with vivid, off-the-beaten-track celebrations of Turkish food culture at its most delicious. Manages to be soulful, inquisitive and thrillingly unpretentious all at once. No one does it like Has."—**Jimi Famurewa**

"A Bourdain-like journal of an identity-affirming journey. So many delicious details, written with care and love."—**Mike Davies, The Camberwell Arms**

"A vivid look into the extensively diverse world of Turkish food: a cuisine we thought we knew, yet Semay's wondrous dive shows us so much more."
– Riaz Phillips

"An incredible insight into exploring identity through food. Hasan has smashed it once again."
– Allan Mustafa, Taste Cadets

"Turkish food through Has' lense; championing humble, honest, real food with bold flavors. Salivating!"—**Ozlem Warren, author of *Sebze***

"Every dish in this book tells a story, and Hasan has done an incredible job showcasing the beauty of Turkish culture through food."—**Gennaro Contaldo**

Praise for *HOME*:

"Outrageously delicious, addictive food cooked with big love and attitude. Books like this come quite rarely ... His ability to cook is phenomenal. [*HOME*] reminds me of my first book."
—Jamie Oliver, BBC *The Food Program*

"[*Big Has: HOME*] is an unfiltered masterclass in the best things in life, namely hero ingredients blasted with searing heat and canny flavors that make life-affirming platefuls. You'd be mad to miss it."
—Great British Food Awards 10 Best Cookbooks of 2022

First published in 2026 by
Interlink Books
An imprint of Interlink Publishing Group, Inc.
46 Crosby Street
Northampton, Massachusetts 01060
www.interlinkbooks.com

Published simultaneously in Great Britain by Pavilion,
An imprint of *HarperCollinsPublishers*

Library of Congress Cataloging-in-Publication
Data available
ISBN 978-1-62371-570-0

This book contains FSC™ certified paper and other controlled sources to ensure responsible forest management.

Publishing Director: Laura Russell
Commissioning Editor: Ellen Simmons
American Edition Editor: Leyla Moushabeck
Design Manager: Alice Kennedy-Owen
American Edition Cover Design: Harrison Williams
Production Controller: Grace O'Byrne
Photographer: Haarala Hamilton
Food Styling: Hasan Semay, Jessica Geddes
Prop Styling: Charlie Phillips
Copyeditor: Vicky Orchard
Sensitivity Reader: Meltem Mete
Proofreader: Anne Sheasby
American Edition Proofreader: Jane Bugaeva
Indexer: Ruth Ellis
Reproduction: Tim Anderson, Rival Color LTD

Printed and bound in China by RR Donnelley APS

WHEN USING KITCHEN APPLIANCES PLEASE ALWAYS FOLLOW THE MANUFACTURER'S INSTRUCTIONS